Darling, I'm Going to *Charlie*

Darling,
I'm Going to *Charlie*

A Memoir

MARYSE WOLINSKI

Translated by H. J. Stone

37INK

—

ATRIA

NEW YORK   LONDON   TORONTO   SYDNEY   NEW DELHI

ATRIA BOOKS · 37INK
An Imprint of Simon & Schuster, Inc.
1230 Avenue of the Americas
New York, NY 10020

Copyright © 2016 by Éditions du Seuil
Originally published in France in 2016 as *Chérie, je vais chez Charlie* by Éditions du Seuil
Published by arrangement with Éditions du Seuil, S.A.
English translation © 2017 by H. J. Stone

First 37 Ink/Atria Books hardcover edition February 2017

37INK / **ATRIA** BOOKS and colophon are trademarks of Simon & Schuster, Inc.

For information about special discounts for bulk purchases, please contact Simon & Schuster Special Sales at 1-866-506-1949 or business@simonandschuster.com.

The Simon & Schuster Speakers Bureau can bring authors to your live event. For more information, or to book an event, contact the Simon & Schuster Speakers Bureau at 1-866-248-3049 or visit our website at www.simonspeakers.com.

Interior design by Kyoko Watanabe

Manufactured in the United States of America

10 9 8 7 6 5 4 3 2 1

Library of Congress Control Number: 2016373566

ISBN 978-1-5011-5489-8
ISBN 978-1-5011-5491-1 (ebook)

Dans mon chagrin rien n'est en mouvement
J'attends personne ne viendra
Ni de jour ni de nuit
Ni jamais plus de ce qui fut moi-même.

—Paul Éluard, *"Ma morte vivante"*
in *Le temps déborde*

Darling, I'm Going to *Charlie*

1

WEDNESDAY, JANUARY 7. I open my eyes and daylight begins to chase away the darkness. My mind hovers for a moment between consciousness and the world of dreams. I listen to the muted sounds in the apartment. The wind whistling in the fireplace. A ray of light crosses the ceiling, a car passes by the building. In the hallway, I can make out the sound of footsteps gliding along the floor: Georges is already up. Will I jump out of bed to hold him tight, or wait for him to push open my bedroom door and come to me?

This man, who is mad about women—their bodies, their audacity, their voices, their fashion, their courage, their faith in whatever they decide, their strong character—this man has looked at me for forty-seven years, lovingly. A look that is penetrating and deeply moving. A look that inspires longing, confidence, a desire to live, a desire to love. A look that makes you addicted to it. A look that sometimes causes reproach: "Why are you looking at me?" Always the same reply: "Guess!" An almost daily ritual. At dinnertime, for example: I'm rushing everywhere in the kitchen, coming and going around him as he calmly sits with a glass of Bordeaux; I bring the first course, go back to the stove to prepare the rest, and he never takes his eyes off me. Annoyed, I burst out: "I can't take a single step without feeling your eyes on me—why?" "Guess!" Or another time, in his office: Him sitting at his drawing board, me on the other side. I speak to him, he looks at me, I know he isn't listening. Risqué images rush through his head, while I very seriously ask his advice on something topical. "You look at me but don't listen." He laughs and holds me close. Furious, I pull away, turn my back on him, and walk out of the room. In the mirror above the fireplace, I follow his gaze, which is fixed on my hips. But now that look is gone. And I hear his voice: "Guess!"

Was he already sitting at his drawing board that morning, finishing the page he would take to the *Charlie Hebdo* editorial meeting? On Wednesdays, the "Charlies" meet to put together the next issue. Well . . . nothing is ever certain with Georges.

He doesn't always go to the Wednesday meetings. If he hasn't finished his drawing in time, he calmly completes it, leaning over his table, in his bathrobe, his hair a mess, his eyes riveted to the sheet of paper. He's not the only one. According to him, Cabu sometimes doesn't show up for *Charlie*'s little team meetings. Bernard as well. The multitalented Bernard Maris; they call him Uncle Bernard. As for the others, I don't really know them. I read only Laurent Léger's articles and Philippe Lançon's juicy columns. I also feel great affection for Cavanna, not just because he discovered Georges's talent, but also because of the values he so fiercely defended. A year before, Cavanna had been taken away by Parkinson's disease, his final companion, the one he had known so well how to dramatize.

It's the first editorial meeting of the year. Georges told me that Charb, the editor in chief, had asked that all the contributors be present. They were going to share an Epiphany cake, and undoubtedly use the occasion to discuss the catastrophic financial situation of the paper and its future, which was far from certain. I remember having asked Georges one day: "What would it mean to you if *Charlie Hebdo* closed?" He shook his head. I thought that my question wasn't very welcome, given his sadness after he'd left the *Journal du Dimanche* the June before, a rejection that had remained without explanation. I insisted nonetheless, and he finally answered. "For fifty years, we've always managed to land on our feet, and we've had many hard times at the paper. We'll find a sponsor, a subsidy, so we can keep our head above water." He didn't really convince me. I could see by his worried look, his weary tone of voice, that something was wrong. Salaries weren't always paid at the end of the month, and even if the check came, he had to wait a while before putting it in the bank. Where had those glorious years gone, the 1980s, when Choron would give everyone a raise whenever he felt like it? I could tell that Georges was worried about the paper's situation. But he put up with it. And he missed the fraternal, jovial atmosphere at *Charlie Hebdo* when Reiser, Gébé, Cavanna, and Choron were there.

At four o'clock, he planned to meet me to view an apartment, since we had agreed to leave our current one, which we liked so much. We had been happy there, in our fashion. We'd moved in six years before, with the idea of staying as long as possible. Neither of us liked being thrown out of our nest. We are at a disadvantage when it comes to moving. In forty-seven years, we've had only three apartments. We didn't want to move any more. But a few months before, our landlord had decided otherwise. He was taking the apartment back for his son. In the place before, where we had lived for thirty-five years, that owner had also announced one fine day: "I'm taking it back for my son." A real wrench. We'd left our youth there.

And so today, the same scenario was being played out. Toward which horizon should we fly? We dealt with it very halfheartedly; we had no desire to leave the plane trees lining the boulevard. Me in particular. Opening the windows and seeing trees was like being in the countryside. For Georges, it was the layout of the place that he'd grown attached to. But actually he could live anywhere, as long as he had his drawing board, the one he went to the United States to buy, for it was "only in the United States that they know how to design drawing boards"—at least the ones he liked. I remember the day he came back from Washington, his board folded under one arm, a suitcase under the other. He was mad with joy.

After getting washed, I rushed into the kitchen to get my breakfast ready. I had only had a few hours' sleep, as usual. But that never stops me from getting a good start to the new day. Perhaps we'd visit the apartment of our dreams, along the quayside. Up to now, we'd seen only pictures of it. Actually, we had already decided: the apartment we'd seen on Monday afternoon that looked out over a boulevard. The real estate agent couldn't find the electricity meter, so we'd looked around in the semidarkness. But we liked everything: the layout of the rooms, which worked with the way we lived and worked, the high windows—two apartments in one, a balcony for my flowers, plane trees below, and undoubtedly a flood of light pouring in during the daytime. We were considering signing the lease quickly. We had a very nice lifestyle, too nice, and since we'd sold our second homes and never thought about how much money we spent, we would be renters for life. Who cares! We loved each other.

Footsteps in the hallway coming closer. This time, it really is him: Georges, my Georges. He comes in, wrapped in his black terry cloth bathrobe; on the back, it says, "My very own Zenith." From the name of the TV program on Canal Plus he worked on with Michel Denisot. Georges drags his feet a little and walks bent over, as if he were carrying the weight of some heavy, guilty secret. Sometimes I catch him walking like that, like an old man, and I wonder what is worrying him so much. Is he suffering because he isn't completely like everyone else, because he is an artist, a real one, so often on the margins of reality? Does he have secrets? That question gnaws at me. This morning, more than ever, his eyes are looking inward, and his thoughts are buried inside him. "Are you all right, darling?" He mumbles a yes, which means both yes and no. Then he picks up the coffeepot and says: "And you? Did you sleep?" "Yes . . .

Well, no, as usual." "Did you go to bed late?" "Yes, too late, the meeting went on forever. Why didn't I get a loving Post-it note last night when I got home?"

The Post-its tell our whole story. They cover the back wall of the kitchen. They speak of his love, his tenderness, his joy when everything is going well, his sadness when his troubles increase. Recently, the fact that his daughters were distant upset him. My women friends envied me for these little notes that came so often. It's true that last night, I was disappointed not to find one on the table in the hall. Tuesday night's Post-it. Too tired to think of it? These past weeks, I've found him morose, lost in his thoughts, his eyes dull. "Is it because of the apartment?" "No, no, it's good, actually, to have a change. We'll try to make some savings and we'll start a new life . . . I think about your future a lot. When I'm no longer here . . ." I sing my old favorite song again: "Instead of dwelling on it, you'd be better off doing something. Is it what's happening at *Charlie Hebdo* that's bothering you?"

He puts down the coffeepot and reaches out to me, and his only reply is to stroke my cheek. While I get my breakfast tray ready, he sits down with his awful milky coffee and dips his bread, dripping with butter and jam, into it. Then we open our datebooks and compare our days. I remind him about the appointments we have together. On this occasion, this January 7, we're viewing the apartment on the quayside. "Can you see yourself living there?" he suddenly asks. "No, I prefer the one on the boulevard." "Well then, why are we going?" "Georges, I've made the appointment, and we have to see more than one before deciding." He gets up, comes back with the newspaper, *Le Monde*. He reads an article out loud, then comments on it. These morning meetings are often my favorite part of the day. But today he's in a hurry. The critique will be short. Before leaving the kitchen, he blows me a kiss and goes to get ready.

"Darling, I'm going to *Charlie*!" he says a few minutes later, shouting from the other end of the apartment. Then he returns, pulls back the curtain that separates my bedroom from the bathroom, and pops his head inside. "Darling, I'm going to *Charlie*." It must be nine o'clock, I'm late, still wrapped in my bath towel, not paying much attention to him. I recall thinking that he was leaving earlier than usual for a *Charlie* meeting. I hear his footsteps in the hallway, then the door slam shut. At that moment, I always feel slightly sad. But today, I know we're going to see each other again that afternoon, at four o'clock.

2

AT TEN O'CLOCK, I go to my Wednesday exercise class. I didn't tell Georges about my concerns over the possible closure of *Charlie Hebdo*. I know that, for him, such a decision would mark the end of a long, great adventure that started when he came back from the Algerian War. Even if he is not always in agreement with certain ideas, certain polemics developed in the newspaper, even certain caricatures, he remains, and would always remain, loyal. He left *L'Humanité* and *Le Nouvel Obser-vateur*, but he would never leave *Charlie Hebdo* as long as the paper existed. Reiser died, then Gébé, then finally Cavanna, in 2014. Each time, he lost a brother. Now the death of the paper itself threatens to strike him. Why can't *Charlie* get readers? Is it an effect of the way society is evolving, which leaves Georges so perplexed? Fifty years of fighting for freedom of expression just to be faced with uneducated people, barbarism, and Sharia law. Once again forced to ask the question "Is it possible to laugh at everything?" Georges chose his camp: the laughter of resistance.

All this is going through my head while I'm trying to relax my body. Eleven o'clock and the class finishes. I head for a meeting and turn off my cell phone.

Around eleven fifteen, on rue Nicolas-Appert, Thomas, an actor and director, is loading scenery onto a truck parked in the alleyway of the Comédie Bastille theater, opposite number 10; it's scenery from the play he directed and acted in for several months, *Visiting Mister Green*. He's in a hurry to load the truck; another theater in Avignon is expecting him for a meeting. It's about to snow, and the journey looks as though it will be difficult. Nathalie, the dresser at the theater, as well as Julien, the stage manager, are giving him a hand. The evening before, they sadly watched the last performance of the play, which never really found its audience. Thomas stays inside the truck while Nathalie and Julien go back and forth to load the various pieces of scenery. A black Citroën races out of the boulevard Richard-Lenoir and onto the street, its tires screeching. Startled, Thomas sticks his head out of the truck; the driver of the car is staring at him. Thomas will never forget the way he looks at him, like a wild animal.

Like Thomas, Joseph, a worker from a nearby construction site, observes the car that parks at the corner of the allée Verte and the rue Nicolas-Appert. Doors slamming and shouting. Surprised, Joseph, like Nathalie and Julien, goes out to see what's happening. They all can see, more or less clearly, three men in black balaclavas coming out of the Citroën. The first man, the driver, is talking with the other two, who are armed with assault weapons and wearing bulletproof vests and extra cartridges slung over their shoulders. Their voices are loud, shrill, but no one understands what they're saying. Thomas thinks he should call the police, but something tells him that if they move, they will be putting their lives in danger. "Are they the GIGN?" Nathalie asks. Thomas and Julien also think it's some kind of GIGN operation, even though they know that the French counterterror police units never go out in such small numbers.

The two armed men head for 6, allée Verte. The third, the driver, visibly unarmed but wearing a bulletproof vest and a balaclava to hide his face, disappears—but Nathalie, Thomas, and Julien don't notice. "Something's happening at *Charlie Hebdo*," Thomas says. All three of them hide behind the truck. Nathalie, a fan of *Charlie Hebdo* when she was young, is surprised. "Is that where they work?" she asks. "There was a police van watching the building until November," Thomas adds. His last words are drowned out by the sound of gunfire inside number 6.

The three friends barricade themselves inside the theater, where they find Marie-France, the manager. "Two armed men went into the building across the street," Nathalie explains. "I hope they're not going to *Charlie Hebdo*," says Marie-France. "What did the armed men look like?" "Like the GIGN. We thought they were GIGN." "Are you dreaming? If it were the GIGN, the streets in the area would be blocked off and dozens of police cars would already be here. We'd hear their sirens. *Charlie Hebdo* is in danger. They've received threats. I even think that one of them had a fatwa put on him. At least, that's what it said in the papers." "You'd think that given the circumstances," Thomas adds, "the place would be protected, barricaded." "What about the police van that's been there since they moved in?" asks Marie-France. "It's been gone since early December," Thomas replies. "That's unbelievable! Why?" Thomas doesn't know what to say. Preoccupied by his play, he hasn't really paid much attention to the news recently, but he did notice the police van had gone and found it strange that it should disappear at the very moment when the newspapers and radio stations were endlessly warning people about the possibility of a new terrorist attack in the capital. "Are you sure?" Nathalie asks again. "First they removed the protective barriers," Thomas remembers, "then the police van stopped coming." What if they were terrorists? This idea gnaws at him. Several rounds of gunfire make them stop talking. A lull, followed by another salvo. "I'm calling the police!" Marie-France returns to her office to dial the emergency services.

Laurent, the production manager for the press agency Premières Lignes, was out on the sidewalk smoking when he heard the first deafening shot echo in the silent street. He saw the backs of two men dressed in black carrying what he knew were military weapons. While they were going in through the allée Verte, he took the stairs in 10, rue Nicolas-Appert and went back up to his office on the second floor, opposite *Charlie Hebdo*, to warn his colleagues and, more important, to call the police. On the phone, he told them about the men in black, who were armed and wearing balaclavas. He himself was unaware that *Charlie Hebdo*'s offices were on the same floor as his office. Their door was marked LES EDITIONS ROTATIVE. Despite the threats received by the newspaper that had been reported in the media, no sign existed in the building to warn people that the satirical publication was located there. Laurent warned the other journalists from the agency. Some of them had already run into Georges and Cabu in the corridors, or had taken the elevators with them. They knew perfectly well that *Charlie Hebdo* was located there. They immediately realized that the armed men were looking for the paper's offices and reproached themselves for never having asked for their phone numbers. How could they warn them? Walk across the hall and knock on the door? Laurent remembered that in the middle of September, one of the journalists from the press agency had been smoking outside on the street when a car stopped in front of him. The driver shouted: "Is this where they find it funny to criticize the Prophet?" The journalist didn't reply. Then the driver added: "You can tell them we're watching them." The journalist took down the car's license plate number and gave the information to Franck Brinsolaro, Charb's bodyguard. Franck sent the information to his superiors at the SDLP.* But protection for *Charlie Hebdo* still hadn't been increased. They had tried to identify the driver, but it had

---

*The SDLP is a protection unit that is part of the French equivalent of the US Department of Homeland Security. [Translator's note]

been decided he had nothing to do with terrorism. Now he's supposedly in a psychiatric facility.

Worried over the increasing amount of gunfire, Laurent tells his colleagues to go up to the roof using the stairs inside the building.

At eleven o'clock, Chantal, an executive saleswoman in her fifties who works for a Swiss company, steps into 10, rue Nicolas-Appert. She is just in time for her meeting at SAGAM, a company that specializes in childcare products. She is welcomed into the company's office, on the ground floor of the building. After the usual introductions, she is shown the room where the meeting she will speak at will be held. To get there, she has to pass 6, allée Verte, the road that cuts through to rue Nicolas-Appert. On the first floor are strollers, changing tables, and all sorts of products for very young children. One of her colleagues is already there.

Suddenly they hear screams from below, followed by a burst of gunfire. Virginie, SAGAM's artistic director, has seen two men dressed in black, and she and another colleague have tried to lock the company's doors. But the men have still gotten inside, and one of them fires into the air, asking the two women where *Charlie Hebdo*'s offices are. Chantal and her colleague don't even have time to answer when one of the two masked men points his Kalashnikov at Chantal's head. The other man stays at the door. Thinking they are being robbed, her colleague takes off his watch and hands it to the armed man, who angrily pushes him away. "Who are you, at *Charlie*?" he asks Chantal. She can't speak. She is convinced she is going to die. She is thinking about her children. She is the loving cornerstone of her family. She imagines them hearing the news that she is dead. She can feel their pain as her fearful eyes never leave the hateful look of the armed man who, for a second, has taken off his balaclava. Despite her terror, Chantal notices that his head is closely shaven. Virginie hears Kouachi's question and screams down the staircase that *Charlie Hebdo* isn't in that building. "You've got the wrong place, it's on the other side, at number ten!" The man looks all around at the strollers and cradles, then turns around, holding his Kalashnikov in front of him, and goes back down the stairs to the ground floor. Petrified, Chantal slumps down onto the table in front of her. She is shaking all over. With great effort, she rushes from the room, followed by her colleague. They go down to the ground floor and try to take refuge in the SAGAM offices. One of the company's executives immediately calls the police. He gives details over the phone: "The man is wearing a balaclava and he's carrying an assault weapon and perhaps a Kalashnikov." Chantal is definite on that point. He adds that the man has an accomplice and they are looking for *Charlie Hebdo*'s offices. He hangs up, and the seven people who are currently in the office build a strong barricade against the entrance before hiding, as best they can, under the desks, fearing the return of the men, whom they immediately identify as terrorists.

The Kouachi brothers then go back across 6, allée Verte and head for 10, rue Nicolas-Appert. They continue to calmly walk down the street in their balaclavas, carrying assault weapons. Frédéric Boisseau, a maintenance man from Sodexo, a food services company, is working at number 10, as he does every day. At this moment, he is chatting with one of his colleagues, Claude Boutant, when a man comes in and asks where he can find *Charlie Hebdo*. Frédéric doesn't have time to reply: a bullet from the Kalashnikov takes his life. The killers go inside the building while Claude Boutant, after seeing that his colleague is dead, quickly pulls out his phone and calls the police.

Taking the inside corridor that links 6, allée Verte to 10, rue Nicolas-Appert, the two men get lost, grow angry, and start shouting. When they get to the floor where there is a sewing company, they come across a postwoman who has just delivered a registered letter. She is terrified, staring at the guns pointed at her. "We're not going to hurt you," says one of the killers. "Where is *Charlie Hebdo*?" She does not reply. Still seeking their prey, the two men climb up to the third floor.

Fang Hui Wang has left his office in the Bayoo company and is smoking a cigarette. It is cold that morning, so he wraps himself up in his jacket. Suddenly he hears shouting behind him. He turns around and finds himself face-to-face with the killers. To impress him, one of them fires into the hallway, toward the offices of another company, the Atelier des Archives. The bullet goes straight through one of the offices and flies out the window. Fang Hui Wang doesn't know where *Charlie*'s offices are, so the killers walk up and down the hallway, more and more stirred up. They come across an executive from another company who also doesn't know, who doesn't even know the newspaper has offices in the building.

———

Still crouching beneath a desk, Chantal wants to warn her husband. It is eleven thirty. She doesn't want him to hear what's happening on the radio or on television. Another gunshot echoes, making the windows and the thin walls of the building, owned by the city of Paris, shake. This time, they didn't fire into the air. Someone has just been killed. Where? No one dares move. Chantal's hand is shaking so hard that it takes her an extremely long time to compose the text message to her husband. She tells him that the police have been warned and will soon arrive. The text is sent at 11:32.

After they too had barricaded themselves behind their flimsy door that didn't even have a sturdy lock, the journalists from Premières Lignes took refuge on the roof of the building. From above, Sylvain, one of the members of the agency, has the idea of warning a policeman whom he knows is responsible for protecting *Charlie Hebdo*. He manages to reach him and explain what is happening. The officer says that he is off duty but that his colleagues will soon be there. Sylvain panics: How can the team at *Charlie* be warned? Other journalists from Premières Lignes have stayed inside the office. They are listening and watching what is happening across the corridor through their peephole.

In the *Charlie Hebdo* offices, the editorial meeting is coming to an end. Around two rectangular tables set up in the narrow room, almost everyone is there, as Charb had requested. But a few of them are away: Patrick Pelloux, an emergency room doctor and journalist, is at a meeting with firemen;

Antonio Fischetti is at his uncle's funeral; Gérard Biard is in London; the illustrator Catherine Meurisse, as well as Zineb, the Moroccan journalist, are on vacation; and Luz has been celebrating his birthday with his sweetheart since dawn.

Nevertheless, there are many around the table to start the New Year in 2015. As usual, the conversation has been lively. Bernard Maris and Philippe Lançon argue about Michel Houellebecq's new novel, *Submission*. That morning, the writer had been interviewed on France Inter on Patrick Cohen's show *Le 7/9*. He had mentioned, somewhat ironically, the police surveillance of Charb and the newspaper. A few months after the attack, in an interview for *Le Figaro*, Houellebecq would say: "When you try not to think irrationally, you start imagining things, wondering how fate relishes so many astonishing configurations of events. This configuration was a tragic one . . . I was caught up in a mechanism of coincidences organized by some unknown intelligence."

Arguments and shouting matches are a tradition at *Charlie Hebdo*, a legacy from its former life as the publication *Hara-Kiri*. And at the editorial meeting, which started with Houellebecq's book, they end up talking about the French jihadists, wondering what the French authorities were doing, faced with such a worrying phenomenon. How could terrorism take root in our country? Bloodbaths, beheadings—that's what led a certain fringe element of the population to become radicalized, especially in the suburbs of Paris.

The suburbs . . . Tignous knows them well. When he is present, better not talk nonsense. So they cross swords, argue, like the freemen they were. That day, like all the others. But they soon have to stop arguing: it is time to share the Epiphany cake and the marble cake that Sigolène has brought. It is eleven thirty; a drawing by Honoré is posted on Twitter, sending *Charlie Hebdo*'s best wishes to Abu Bakr al-Baghdadi, the head of ISIS.

Coco, the illustrator, suggests to Angélique, the receptionist, that they go outside for a cigarette. Wrapped up in their parkas, carrying a pack of cigarettes and a lighter, they leave. Inside, everyone starts collecting his or her things. After a chat with Simon, the newspaper's webmaster, Georges does the same, according to the surveillance camera in the newspaper's reception area. Philippe Lançon already has his pea jacket on and is ready to leave when he suddenly changes his mind: he wants to show Cabu a book on jazz, *Blue Note*, which contains black-and-white photos from the 1950s and '60s.

Maryse Wolinski

Like Georges, Jean Cabu is mad about jazz. I imagine him opening his sparkling eyes wide, fascinated by the photos of Miles Davis, John Coltrane, Thelonious Monk, among others, the people who so successfully played jazz back then. Philippe explains that he is going to write an article on that magnificent book that afternoon. For now, he's in a hurry, he has to leave. Cabu puts on his duffel coat and invites his friend Michel Renaud, the president of the Rendez-vous du carnet de voyage festival held at Clermont-Ferrand, to share the Epiphany cake with them. This is the first time that Michel Renaud has been to one of the editorial meetings. He'd come to return some sketches to Cabu, and he confirmed a date with Georges for a future festival. Philippe then goes to put the book in his bag, which he'd left at the other end of the room. Charb is chatting with his bodyguard, Franck Brinsolaro, who has come to the meeting. Since the fire at the former offices and the fatwa placed on him, sent through the jihadist media, Charb had been given protection: first, three men armed with handguns, then, a few months later, reduced to two. Charb and Franck, his "backup" as they say in police jargon, get along well. They often have lunch together at the Petites Canailles, the restaurant where the Charlies are regulars and where Georges so wanted to take me. At first, I always refused, since I didn't know the Charlies well. After two years of "living together," Charb suggested that Franck come to the editorial meetings. And he agreed. He is not around the table, of course, but sitting a bit behind. After seeing one of the front covers Charb has drawn, he often tells his colleagues at the Protection Unit that it will "cause a shit storm." He knows that the threats are intensifying, which is why Charb is on level two surveillance, a high level on the scale of four. Charb's second bodyguard has gone out to buy a sandwich on the rue Richard-Lenoir.

As Coco and Angélique walk down the stairs, they are surprised to hear shouting at the front of the building. They find themselves face-to-face with the two armed men. "You're Coco, and you're gonna take us to *Charlie Hebdo*," one of them orders. "And you," the other one says to Angélique, "you stay here." What is going through Coco's mind, a Kalashnikov pointed at her head, ordered to take men she understands to be terrorists into the paper's office, while she is supposed to soon go and pick up her child from the nursery? Without a doubt, she is terribly torn, something only she knows, because, out of decency, no one has asked her that question. She thinks she can stall while taking them to the third floor. Her legs are shaking as she climbs the stairs, the gun still pointed at her head. "Where's *Charlie Hebdo*?" the man in black shouts. On the office door, there is no mention of the satirical newspaper, just the name LES EDITIONS ROTATIVE. The men grow impatient, their gestures more violent. On the second floor, Coco stops in front of a door with an electronic entry system. The man tells her to enter the code. At that moment, did she think about her child, like Chantal? About her colleagues and friends who are in the room, about to share the Epiphany cake? Her colleagues and friends who are about to be assassinated. Coco enters the code.

Édouard, a journalist at Premières Lignes, is still hiding with some of his colleagues. They take turns watching what is happening in the corridor by looking through the peephole. They hear screams. The men in black that Édouard saw are ordering a woman they are calling Coco to enter the code to open the door. Édouard and the others do not know Coco. Édouard has run into Cabu and Georges several times, but he has never really gotten to know the team. The journalists understand what is about to happen. They see the two men in black in the corridor about to go into *Charlie Hebdo*'s offices. Édouard has the idea of setting off the fire alarm but changes his mind, thinking it might provoke a catastrophe. He calls the police again, repeating his remarks. At that moment, eleven calls have already reached the police, who send the information to all the officers on duty.

Eleven calls, all saying the same thing: *Charlie Hebdo*, the masked men with assault weapons.

The first call was made at 11:18 by Claude Boutant, the maintenance man, after the terrorists killed Frédéric Boisseau, his colleague. The second call was made by the manager of SAGAM. Then a call from the manager at the Atelier des Archives, located on the third floor of 6, allée Verte, where the killers got lost before returning to 10, rue Nicolas-Appert. At 11:29, one of the journalists from Premières Lignes tried (in vain) to call the police. The number was busy. Other calls would be sent from the building opposite number 10. Yet nothing stopped the men in black from getting into the newspaper's offices.

It appears that at 11:25, a patrol of police officers on bicycles in the 11th arrondissement intercepted a first message and headed for the rue Nicolas-Appert, before receiving a second message. Gunshots were reported heard on the rue Nicolas-Appert, with no other details. The first messages the police received did not mention the name of the newspaper. At about

11:25, the police at the headquarters in the 11th arrondissement received a radio message from BAC, the Anticrime
Squad, which was already there and was asking for backup,
saying it was an emergency, but without providing further
details. At about 11:27, the police informed the emergency
services that gunshots were heard at 10, rue Nicolas-Appert.
Charlie Hebdo was still not mentioned.

At 11:33, according to the surveillance camera in the reception area, the front door gives way after being violently forced
open. A first man in black, wearing a balaclava and carrying
an assault weapon, bursts in shouting *"Allahu akbar!"* followed
by another armed man dressed the same. The first man pushes
the distraught Coco against a wall and fires at Simon Fieschi,
the newspaper's webmaster, who had quickly gotten out of
his chair; he immediately falls to the floor, fatally wounded.
The editorial office is about two yards away. No obstacles, no
protection. No doors that need keycards to open them. One of
the killers stays in the tiny space that serves as the reception
area while the other one kicks open the door, again shouting
"Allahu akbar!" Then he moves forward and asks: "Where
is Stéphane Charbonnier?" using Charb's real name. Then
he fires, and fires again. One bullet after the other. Everyone, illustrators and journalists, each fall in turn, in silence,

without screaming, killed by the terrorists: Charb, Georges, Cabu, Tignous, Honoré, Elsa Cayat, Bernard Maris. Franck Brinsolaro, Charb's bodyguard, pulls out his gun, in vain. Even though he was always on the alert, he didn't hear the first gunshots fired at the entrance to the building that killed the maintenance man, Frédéric Boisseau, because the office doors are reinforced. Laurent Léger is at the far end of the conference table. He has the time, and the presence of mind, to throw himself under the little table reserved for Charb's security detail, and he doesn't move. Riss and Fabrice Nicolino, other journalists who have been wounded, pretend they're dead. The smell of gunpowder fills the room. At the back of the office, Philippe Lançon collapses. He is still holding the book on jazz. He is alive, but seriously wounded, a bullet in his jaw. Like his friends, he pretends to be dead. Sigolène, stunned by what has just happened to her, has forgotten about the coffee she had left to make in the alcove next to the editorial room. When the killers burst in, she had thrown herself to the ground and had started crawling, eyes closed. Hidden now behind a little wall that separates the offices, she listens and hears nothing but gunfire. But soon she hears footsteps; one of the killers is getting closer. She sees black legs coming toward her. Mustapha, the copyeditor, who also threw himself to the ground, has just been found. Another gunshot. The man walks forward a little and sees Sigolène. He goes around the wall and aims his gun at her. Seeing the killer's eyes and the Kalashnikov, she starts shaking and bursts into tears. But it seems that the man with the "gentle expression" is troubled. "Don't be afraid. Calm down. I'm not going to kill you. Don't worry, we don't kill women, but think about what you're doing, because what you're doing is bad. I will spare you on condition that you read the Koran." His voice is hoarse, hesitant. She will hear that voice for a long time after the event, just as she will find it difficult to forget the way he looked at her. The man then turns toward the editorial room, where his accomplice is continuing the massacre. "We don't kill women!" he shouts, three times. Despite her terror, Sigolène thinks about Jean-Luc, the layout artist, who is hiding behind his desk. Before the Kouachi brothers got inside, Jean-Luc had heard the first gunshots fired, and, thinking it was a bomb, had lain down under his desk on the other side of the glass panel that separates the conference room from the other spaces reserved for the administrators and editors. Sigolène thinks the killer hasn't seen him. Meanwhile, the other man continues shooting.

"Good, we got Charb." Laurent can hear the voice of the man who calmly, coldly, executed his friends. "We got them all," replies the second man, who had come as backup. It is 11:35. The killers have completed their mission. They leave the *Charlie Hebdo* offices.

Jean-Luc hears the sound of the killers' footsteps on the staircase. He knows that once he stands up, he will see the horrific scene. *They're all dead*, he thinks, then has the faint hope that some of them may be only wounded and that he may be able to help them.

The impudent pens of the press became the targets of religious fundamentalists. They tried to kill laughter, that powerful force of opposition. But as my daughter, Elsa, wrote in a letter to her father, published in *Elle* magazine, "they killed the man, but not the ideas." They killed all that talent, but their ideas will continue to spread. The bicycle patrol that would arrive on the scene after the Anticrime Squad, just before the terrorists left number 10, would again call for backup. It wasn't until 11:40 that a radio message would state that gunshots had been heard near the *Charlie Hebdo* offices. At the same time, the local police squad from the 11th arrondissement would be informed as well. But it would be too late.

3

A DEATHLY SILENCE lingers over the *Charlie Hebdo* offices for several minutes—a horrifying "white noise," as Laurent would later recall. Suddenly, the ones who escaped being killed hear gunfire in the distance. Outside, the men in black are firing at the police. Jean-Luc, the layout artist, decides to stand up. Cécile, the manager of *Charlie*'s publishing house, Les Échappés, is near him. He'd seen his colleague grab Luce, a specialist in ecology and animals, and watched the two women hide under the desks. After Jean-Luc, Sigolène gets up. She sees the horrific scene. Philippe, whose cheek has been ripped apart by a bullet, gestures to her to help him. Two of his friends' bodies are on top of him. Sigolène walks toward him. She wants to lift the corpses off him and give him her hand. She wants to, but, overcome with nausea, she cannot. She then thinks she must immediately call the emergency services and goes to look for her cell phone, which she lost somewhere among the dead bodies. She finally finds it and dials the number, shouting into the phone "It's *Charlie Hebdo*, get here fast, they're all dead!" She then spots Cécile, Luce, and Coco, then Jean-Luc. Safe and sound. They stand and hug each other and wait—for what seems an eternity—for help to come.

The seven people from SAGAM, along with Chantal, are still hiding under the desks, barricaded in; they've heard the gunshots. Someone quietly speaks: "They've murdered *Charlie Hebdo*."

Thomas, Julien, Nathalie, and Marie-France, cornered in the lobby of the theater, have also heard everything. When shouts reach the door of 10, rue Nicolas-Appert, they rush to the window in Marie-France's office and see the two killers raising their Kalashnikovs in the air, shouting "The Prophet Mohammed has been avenged!" In the allée Verte, three policemen arrive on bicycles.

———

It must be 11:45 when Chantal hears the first siren: a police van has just arrived as backup to the Anticrime Squad. The three policemen inside fire at the back of the killers' black Citroen. They are not equipped to fight against the assault weapons of their enemies, and they know it. The car backs into the boulevard Richard-Lenoir, and the policemen take cover.

Ahmed Merabet, a policeman, is in a patrol car in the area not far from where the gunshots aimed at the Anticrime Squad were fired. He gets out of the car. From the window inside the theater, Thomas shouts down to him that two terrorists are leaving the *Charlie Hebdo* offices. Ahmed Merabet fires, takes a bullet to the leg, and tries to save himself by running toward the boulevard Richard-Lenoir.

In the building on the other side of the street, a man has heard everything; he opens his window and starts the video camera on his cell phone. He sees the police officer fall onto the sidewalk, writhing in pain. Two armed men dressed all in black go over to him. One of them gets closer to the wounded man: "So you wanted to kill us, huh?" he sniggers. The policeman tries to get up and begs: "Don't, man, it's OK." The killer aims his Kalashnikov and murders him in cold blood.

The man at the window is beside himself by what he has just witnessed. He immediately posts the video on Facebook. The sight of a murder taking place as it happens would be seen all over the world and cause shock waves in social media. A few minutes later, the video post would be taken down. Today, the man who filmed it calls himself a "hostage" of the events he regrets having filmed. He did not realize the risk he was running. And since then, he can't sleep.

As for the brave Ahmed, he undoubtedly did not have time to think about his mother, with whom he still lived. He had just finishing building a house for the two of them and had sent out invitations to a housewarming party. He was hoping to get a job with the Criminal Investigation Department and had passed the exams with flying colors. He was dreaming of a new project: becoming a lawyer. The assassins killed that dream.

A little while later, Thomas, the actor, sees two men arrive; one of them is holding a camera. Within a few minutes, the street is filled with police officers and journalists. So what exactly happened between the first call, at 11:18, and the moment when the local police became aware of the blood-bath that took place at the threatened newspaper, at 11:40? The commanders of the local Anticrime Squad admitted that they didn't know the *Charlie Hebdo* offices were located at rue Nicolas-Appert, or were even in the area where they worked. They were surely not the only ones. But why wasn't the name of the newspaper mentioned in the first emergency messages?

Is there no communication at all between the Protection Unit and the local police headquarters?

Chantal hears the first police siren at 11:45. It would be followed by many others. Next, a cacophony of sirens. One after the other, the employees from SAGAM emerge from their hiding places. Thirty minutes that would shatter Chantal's life: she became claustrophobic, terrified by the slightest sound, and unable to sleep, and has been on sick leave from work since the attack.

Before getting away, and without seeming in a hurry, one of the two killers picked up the shoe he'd lost while running after Ahmed Merabet and shouted: "Tell the media that we did this for Al-Qaida in Yemen!"

The two men were certainly not lone wolves, as was sometimes reported in the press. They had received orders. A few days after the attack, Al-Qaida in the Arabian Peninsula released a video confirming that it had ordered the *Charlie Hebdo* massacre. Very quickly, investigators traced the accomplices back to people who had already fled to Turkey via Syria. Among them were the Belhoucine brothers. From Turkey, they sent this message to their family: "Don't worry. We have joined the caliphate. We would rather live in a country ruled by Sharia law and not by laws invented by men."

4

AFTER MY MEETING, I decide to take a taxi. At Gobelins station, the driver is very friendly. The blanket of fog has lifted, it's twelve thirty, and I feel good. My meeting with the person I'd long wanted to interview has gone well; I'll now be able to make some progress on the stage play I've been working on for a few months. I decide to go home for lunch before meeting Georges at the quayside. I imagine he is now sharing the delicious Epiphany cake with the Charlies. I also think that in the end, our forthcoming move is a bit of luck, and that even though I was worried when we first found out, I now feel rather good about it. Something a little new, moving forward together as a couple, after forty-seven years at the side of my talented husband. Yes, the idea of moving now makes me feel exhilarated.

I automatically turn on my phone to call Georges and remind him of our appointment. He doesn't answer. Did he forget to switch his phone on after the editorial meeting? I leave him a message. I know he always calls me back the minute he sees my name on the screen. I'm about to put my phone away when I notice I have an awful lot of voicemails. Twenty-five, to be precise, and as many texts, some from friends I haven't seen in months. All in less than an hour? So many calls? I'm confused. I start to read them. "How is Georges?" "Is Georges at home?" "Did Georges go to the *Charlie* meeting?" "Where is Georges?" "Have you heard from Georges?"

I don't understand. I can hear the last words Georges called out to me a few hours earlier, before leaving the apartment: "Darling, I'm going to *Charlie*." So that's where he is. Otherwise, where else could he be? Has something happened to him? "Monsieur," I say to the taxi driver, "I've just turned on my phone and there are a lot of messages, especially from some people I haven't seen in a long time, asking me about my husband." We are now at the Sénat, at the top of the rue Tournon. The driver slows down, pulls over, and turns around to look at me. "Madame, I don't know what your husband does . . . But haven't you heard what's happened?" "No, what's going on?" My heart starts beating faster. "There was a terrorist attack, Madame, and it's serious!" "A terrorist attack? Where? My husband was at his newspaper . . ." "A terrorist attack, Madame, at *Charlie Hebdo*."

I feel as if I no longer inhabit my own body. "We have to go there," I tell him. "I want to see my husband." The driver hesitates and advises against it. "The whole area is already blocked off," he explains. "We'd never get near it." I insist, I absolutely want to see my husband, I want to be with him. The pressure mounts, a strange burning sensation runs through me. My mind is confused. I can't think straight. At that moment, my cell phone rings. Arnauld, my son-in-law, is at 10, rue Nicolas-Appert, the site of the attack. His office was close by, so as soon as he heard about it through social media, he rushed over to *Charlie Hebdo*. "Well? Where is Georges? I want to be with him." I don't let Arnauld speak and he finally cuts in. He agrees with the taxi driver that I should go home and wait for news. "No one knows anything yet." "What do you mean, no one knows anything? That's impossible . . ." I insist again, Arnauld lies to me, I want to see Georges, talk to him, hold him close. "No," says Arnauld. "No, you have to go home." His voice is shaking, with anguish, with fear, and I understand only too well. He hangs up. "Are we going to your place? Madame, please, it makes more sense," the driver insists. "I really hope nothing's happened to your husband." He turns the radio on. Together, we cling to every word of the news, but I hear nothing, understand nothing. Two men armed with Kalashnikovs, gunfire in the *Charlie Hebdo* offices, journalists kept at a distance by the police, and then, nothing more, except a continuous loop about the gunfire, the dead or wounded, and that it was a terrorist attack. "Darling, I'm going to *Charlie*." I remember the last words Georges wrote to me, the day before yesterday: "Darling, I went for some sushi, rue de la Chaise. It's 9:15, I'm going to read for a while and then go to sleep, thinking of you. I'm worried because you do too much and you're tired. I love you, as always." And another message, from a while ago, that I can't forget: "Darling, I'm thinking of you, you are the woman of my dreams. Alas! Life is short. See you tomorrow, I think we're going to the theater (Vieux Co), your husband of 42 years. I love you, G."*

The phone rings again: it's my daughter, her voice is choked up. "Mom, you have to go home, I'm coming over." "Are you at *Charlie Hebdo*?" She's hung up. The phone rings

---

* Also called the Vieux Co, Le Vieux-Colombier is a theater in Paris.

again, just as the taxi heads up the boulevard Raspail. "Do you have any news of Georges?" I have difficulty recognizing the voice of Françoise, a friend of mine who is a judge. "Françoise, we have to find out what happened to Georges, right away." Georges still isn't answering his phone. Françoise tells me not to go to where the attack took place and hangs up very quickly.

We arrive at my building and the driver walks me to the door. He helps me inside. "Madame," he says, tears in his eyes, "I hope nothing has happened to your husband. I'll be thinking of you. I'll pray for you."

What could possibly happen to Georges that wouldn't also happen to me? I stagger up the stairs. I can picture the tears in the taxi driver's eyes, tears I will never forget. It takes me ages to open the door to my apartment. Once inside, I drop my handbag and the documents I'm carrying and think about what Arnauld said. I must sit on the sofa and wait for his call. The idea doesn't even occur to me to turn on the radio or the TV. I pace back and forth in my bedroom, I turn the pages of a manuscript I promised to read, but the words are blurred. I can think only of Georges, his smile, his kisses, his tenderness, Georges who wrote in several of his books that "tenderness is the culmination of love." For him, love had to remain intense, or it didn't exist at all. And he knew how to show his tenderness in so many ways. I am obsessed by one image: Georges in the editorial room. I want to hold him tight, take his face in my hands, kiss him on the mouth. I want to feel his body, alive.

5

AT 12:17, THE Anticrime Squad goes into the SAGAM office, where Chantal and her colleagues have come out of their hiding places. The questions come thick and fast. How many were there of them? How old? What did they look like? What were they wearing? What kind of weapons did they have? Chantal can still feel the barrel of the Kalashnikov against her temple. She can barely speak. She is shaking, pressing her cell phone against her, the link with her husband and children. The link with the life she has just nearly lost. "You can go," says one of the officers, who seems to be in charge. "We'll call you if we need you."

In the street, Chantal comes face-to-face with the emergency service workers, ambulance drivers, firefighters, medics, police officers, journalists, camera operators, photographers, politicians. She passes Manuel Valls, the prime minister, who has taken over from the president at the scene of tragedies. She wonders why they have both come here. Everyone is posing for the cameras in front of 10, rue Nicolas-Appert, but why? To show solidarity? On the second floor, there is a horrific scene; a monstrous attack has taken place. There is nothing more that can be said. The words endlessly repeated in front of the cameras are meaningless.

The area is completely blocked off, and traffic in Paris is almost at a standstill. The arrival of ministers and other officials at the scene has mobilized the police to protect them. From my apartment, I hear the sirens of the motorcades that precede the cortege of government cars. And I still don't know where Georges is and why he hasn't called me. I left him a message, so he should call me back. If he doesn't, it's because he can't. But why? Waiting fills me with pain, confusion, incomprehension. Georges, we have an appointment on the quayside to plan our new life! I'm thinking about the two of us, but now I should be thinking about him, and him alone. Suddenly, a question comes to mind: Why has Arnauld called me and not Georges?

In the theater, Thomas has hunted down a journalist. Even

though they weren't allowed to cross the roped-off area, one of them has sneaked in through the courtyard of the theater and is hiding in the restroom; from the window, he is filming the emergency services personnel rushing around, the groups of police officers and the families who are arriving on the scene. Furious, Thomas kicks him out of his hiding place. He's seen enough today. He knows that in the building opposite, on the second floor, the illustrators he so admired have lost their lives, killed by terrorists. An attack has just taken place at *Charlie Hebdo*, and, he thinks, nothing was done to stop it. It must have been 11:00 when the Kouachi brothers arrived. In spite of the call made at 11:17, why didn't the police get there before the killers made it into the *Charlie* offices? He himself had been an impotent witness. He wants to get away from this hell at all costs. He says good-bye to his team and tells them he's leaving for Avignon. But it is impossible to leave the police perimeter without an escort. A police car accompanies him to the place de la Bastille, allowing him to pass. Completely distraught by what he has just lived through, he heads south.

After Thomas leaves, Nathalie and Julien take refuge inside the theater, where the people labeled "involved" or "survivors" have been brought. They are wearing tags around their necks that say INVOLVED. One of them says that when the police went into the *Charlie* editorial room, they were shocked by the sight of the massacre before their eyes. Devastated, they had difficulty going inside and leaning over the victims. An officer with a loud voice then shouted: "Are there any survivors? Come out!" *Survivors.* Everyone who could has left the offices and is being cared for by the emergency services workers. Then the families of the victims who had come to rue Nicolas-Appert are allowed to go into the theater.

Everywhere people are crying, sobbing, shouting. People want information but nothing is leaked; the police remain silent. Do they know? Are there any instructions? Chloé Verlhac, the wife of the illustrator Tignous, wrapped up in a big scarf, tries to sneak through the crowd of journalists, politicians, ambulance drivers, medics, and police officers to get to the front door of 10, rue Nicolas-Appert. The security men stop her. Like me, she wants to know; she wants to hold her Tignous in her arms and quickly take him home, where their two young children are waiting for them. No, impossible. She can either go to the theater or to the tents set up by the police and the medics. But what she really wants is an answer to her questions: "Where is my Tignous? What happened to him? Is he up there, in the office?" She gets no reply and is asked to move along. Once again, she slips between the police officers to avoid the photographers and journalists who are hovering around the families to get a scoop. And then, just as she steps onto the sidewalk on her way to the theater, someone tells her that ten people are dead and others wounded. She bursts into tears, hides her face in her scarf. Her legs give way. She goes into the theater and waits, takes the glass of water that Nathalie hands her. She waits but can't take it anymore. Then she corners a policeman and orders him to tell her if her Tignous is dead, wounded, or alive. *Alive?* No, she no longer believes that. He would already be there to take her in his arms. "Please, tell me. Tell me." And, amid a crowd of people in tears, she hears the news that he is dead. Nathalie can't believe how coldly it is done, such information casually announced to no one in particular, or nearly. Even though she had suggested to the police that they meet with the families in the empty manager's office. But they didn't follow up.

Hélène, Philippe Honoré's daughter, had been warned by her mother. She had gone to the 11th arrondissement to get more information. Impossible to get near the site. She ended up back on the rue Richard-Lenoir, along with the medics and police officers who barely answered her questions. She sees ambulance drivers go past, carrying stretchers.

One policeman finally feels sorry for this young woman shivering in the freezing cold and sends her to the Red Cross tent. She goes in. They have her sit down, give her a glass of water, and promise to get answers to her questions. "Where is my father? Was he one of the victims? Is he hurt?" Hours go by, with no news. She decides to go into the theater. Perhaps she'll find someone from *Charlie*, a survivor, who can give her information. But waiting is unbearable. She constantly calls her mother, who is glued to the television. For now, no details are being given on any of the channels. She finally makes it onto the sidewalk in front of the theater. The police push her back. "We only allow people who were involved here." At that moment, Anne Hidalgo, the mayor of Paris, surrounded by bodyguards, enters the theater. Hélène can't stand it anymore; she gives vent to her anger and shouts: "They let politicians in but not the families!" Anne Hidalgo has heard her. She turns around and gestures to Hélène to come with her. Inside, politicians are mingling with the "involved" and the members of the *Charlie Hebdo* team who didn't go to the meeting and so are still alive. Hélène rushes over to Jean-Luc, the newspaper's layout artist. He knows. He puts his arm around Hélène and tells her: "Your father is dead, like Wolinski, like Cabu, like Elsa Cayat, like Charb and his bodyguard, like Bernard Maris, like Mourad." Now she too knows. The presence of the "involved," others like Jean-Luc and Laurent, helps her through her pain.

Nathalie is also with her. She is playing psychiatrist, handing out coffee, glasses of water, cigarettes. She would like to hide in the theater manager's office and rest for a few seconds, away from the sobbing, a break from having to calm everyone down, a few minutes when she doesn't have to witness the scenes of distress she is finding harder and harder to deal with, but there is no time. Julien comes to help her; he is also obliged to play psychiatrist. He is listening to people who have a passionate need to speak, to tell their stories, to describe their shock, the shooting, the smell of gunpowder, and the black legs of the killers they saw from the places where they had hidden.

Others are more silent. Sitting on the floor, they cry, their faces buried in their hands. The theater continues to fill up. Nathalie continues serving drinks. She hands a cup of tea to one of the people involved. "Be careful," she says, "it's hot." The man dips his finger into the cup several times, burns himself, and without flinching gulps down the tea. She doesn't know who they are now, the journalists and illustrators from *Charlie Hebdo*, because she doesn't read it anymore. She used to, a while ago, when it was at its height with people like Choron, Cavanna, Wolinski, Cabu, Reiser. She would have recognized them. But she knows they're on the other side of the street, two floors up. Because they're not among the wounded, or the "involved" . . .

But she dare not think about them being dead. Dead, murdered. Because the police van isn't there anymore. She can still remember when the three men in balaclavas arrived, one was the driver and wasn't armed. When interrogated a few days later at the central police station on the quai des Orfèvres, she would detail what she'd seen. According to Nathalie, she would be asked not to mention the third man. Why? The value of her testimony is questioned. Nathalie thinks he must have taken off his balaclava and run away without being seen. Thomas will also say he saw the third man in front of the door at number 10, while the other two were looking for *Charlie Hebdo*. When people panic, their testimony varies. But Nathalie and Thomas are not the only ones to suggest there was a third man. The policemen from the Anticrime Squad would also say they saw three men in balaclavas coming out of number 10.

At three o'clock, when the doctors and psychiatrists arrive, Nathalie feels relieved. She can finally go out into the cold afternoon air and have a cigarette. She needs one, she's hungry, having eaten only the Mars bars, potato chips, and madeleines she found in the theater and shared with the "involved" and their families. There was nothing left. She runs upstairs to look for some blankets for the "involved" who had come down from *Charlie Hebdo* without any of their things; they were starting to shiver in the poorly heated theater. But it is impossible to leave. A policeman stops her. Everyone is kept there until six thirty. A policeman asks Nathalie to go to the central police station. She refuses. She can't take any more and wants to get back to her daughter, who has been on the phone with her constantly and who is worried, knowing she is still at the site of the massacre.

6

IMPOSSIBLE TO SIT down. I walk from my desk to my bed, from the sofa to the chair, I tell myself once more that nothing could happen to Georges, it isn't possible. My thoughts clash, and very quickly my body takes over. I feel as if it is emptying, as if all my organs are breaking off and my brain is no longer functioning. I'm shaking from the cold and my face feels on fire, both at the same time. My legs no longer support me and my arms hang limply at my sides; I drop the telephone I'd been gripping tightly for several minutes. I must pull myself together, at all costs, otherwise I'll miss the call that will give me the news. But I can't. I stagger, my life is turned upside down. My life. Our life; it's disappearing. My teeth are chattering, I'm shaking with cold, fear, anguish, even though I'm still wearing my coat; it never occurred to me to take it off. I put down just my bag, so my hands would be free. I have nothing but physical reactions. One question alone obsesses me: Why hasn't Georges called me back? He was supposed to answer my message and confirm our appointment on the quayside. If he's been wounded, I want to know, and quickly.

Suddenly the phone rings. Where is the damned thing? I rush all around the room. I do not want to believe that I will no longer be able to hold Georges in my arms, that my face will no longer feel the touch of his hand, that he will no longer leave me loving Post-it notes. No, it isn't possible. I finally find the phone on the bedside table. I answer.

I hear a friend's voice: "Where is Georges? Did he call you?" I can't speak. My silence worries her. "Is he . . ." "No, no, I don't know. I don't know anything." "Did anyone tell you what happened? I mean anyone official?" "No one." "The police, the authorities? No? Really, no one? That's unbelievable!" I want her to hang up quickly but she continues: "I heard some of them were just wounded. Let's hope so." "I have to go." "Of course, I'll call you back. Don't worry, it will be all right."

I hold the phone with shaking hands; it rings again. My sister wants to know, I have to tell her the truth. And I say I know nothing. That the waiting is unbearable. I feel as if my brain is on fire. "It isn't possible," she says over the phone. "Impossible, Georges . . ." She hangs up.

I decide not to answer the phone again unless it's Arnauld. I sit down in front of my desk, where the pages of a manuscript are piled high, pages I'll never finish. I look at them and read a few lines, which seem foreign to me. I don't even know what I wrote yesterday. The past has disappeared while I wait, interminably. I force myself to try to remember what Georges and I said to each other yesterday, before I went to my meeting. We must have talked about the apartment we'd visited that we'd liked so much, and about moving and our new life. And just as I was about to leave, I noticed the sad look he always gave me when I was going out for dinner without him. I left the apartment with a heavy heart. Now I want him to call me, I want to hear his voice. My eyes are filled with tears.

The third call is the one I'd been waiting for. It's Arnauld. He is at the theater with the families. I listen to him. His voice is firm, direct: "Georges was murdered. He's dead." "No, no . . . It isn't possible." "It's true. He's dead. Elsa is coming to you." Then he hangs up.

My throat tightens, as if someone is trying to strangle me. I can't breathe. The feeling of being choked paralyzes me. Suddenly I realize what Arnauld has just told me. But how could he know? Who told him? Only the investigators are supposed to have that information. Just as they are supposed to inform the people involved. But the police never contacted me. I received no information at all. Was everyone at *Charlie Hebdo* dead? Since no one tried to contact me, that can't be the case. The fact that I have had no official confirmation drives me mad. Until I hear it from an official source, I can't believe it. Georges, our carefree life, can't end like this. We still have so much life to live together.

———

When my daughter arrived, she too could not understand how this terrible news had not yet been told to us by the authorities. We'd waited all day, but no one had called. I remained seated on the sofa in the living room, shaking all over, body and soul. For twenty-four hours, no tranquilizer worked, not even the one prescribed by a doctor friend of mine whom I'd immediately called for help.

Little by little, the living room of our apartment filled up with people: Georges's daughters with their spouses and children, close friends, another friend of mine who is a doctor, dressed in black and who reminded me of my grandmother when she arrived in Paris, her face half-hidden under a black veil, after her husband had died in Algeria. Each of them sat down beside me and talked to me. I heard nothing, nothing but Georges's voice: "Darling, I'm going to *Charlie*." He had left me only a few hours earlier. Impossible to believe he'd been murdered. Why him? Around me, some people were crying. I had no tears left.

And that was how our life together ended.

7

IN MY SLEEPLESS night, I can hear the rounds from the Kalashnikov and picture the way Georges looked at me, etched in my mind forever, a look of love, of distress. Dressed in black and wearing a balaclava, the trained killer is calm; he aims and fires with no hesitation and no concessions. The first bullet pierces the aorta and heart of my beloved, then his body drops. The other three bullets were pointless. His body, facedown on the ground. Someone else slumps down at his side, a friend, a brother, and then another, and another. Ten would fall from the Kalashnikov's thirty-four bullets. Four would be wounded. The night is very dark, silent, and I know I won't go back to sleep. The sound of gunfire will return to haunt me, keeping me awake. And when I finally drift off, another scenario plays out its scenes of terror.

I see them every night, at around four o'clock, and I start trembling, shaking that won't stop until daybreak. The two terrorists burst in without difficulty, because there are no obstacles, they scream, aim their weapons at the *Charlie Hebdo* team, who are dumbstruck. I try to picture the look on Georges's face, but I can't. It's as if his expression has disappeared. I ask myself questions. No, Georges didn't have time to form any expression at all. His astonishment got the better of him. I prefer that he fell without thinking. Without suffering. I picture it: with his four or five stents, because of his arteriosclerosis, his heart must have failed. A heart attack took him before the terrorists' bullets. From the first day, I tell myself the story of the heart attack. It calms me down. And still, I cannot get back to sleep. Images, shouting, the barrage of bullets, the violence, the bodies falling one on top of the other. And the color red bursts forth like sparks in my eyes. Carnage. Burning into my impossible nights. Why does evil exist? Where does it come from, if not from man himself, then from fanatics convinced they hold the truth? Doesn't a good life consist of seeking the path to truth without ever claiming to possess it?

Humor killed. A few strokes of an impertinent pencil and death at the end of that pencil, or felt-tip, or pen. There will be nothing but anxiety now, because there will never be an answer. Sleepless nights, or endless nightmares. The Kouachi brothers, whose photos I constantly see in the press—the very sight of them is a knife to my heart—scale the facade of my building, break the windows, and murder me the way they executed Georges and his friends. This other scenario began after I received a threatening letter. Nights filled with ever more questions. Nights when I write letters dictated by vengeance and despair. Letters that will never be sent. The slightest word in an article, the least mention on the radio or during a gathering of victims, and I explode, get carried away, give free rein to my anger. As soon as the sun sets on the horizon, wherever I am, I am filled with fear. Georges's eyes have closed forever. I have lost my light, my confidence. Will day break again tomorrow? There is no longer a road ahead of me, only an expanse of happy days or less-happy days between today and the past. Night and day, I must continue to fight without him, without the man who was my support in life.

A war scene in which Georges was killed. These last few years, there have been scenes of war everywhere in the world, on every continent. The fanatics at work. It's bread and but-ter to television and to certain newspapers. But is it possible that such a scene could have taken place in the offices of a satirical newspaper, on the second floor of a peaceful street in Paris? Sleep has abandoned me, once and for all; waking up plunges me into the horror of the massacre. *Massacre* is the word the journalists use over and over again. I turn on the radio and hear: "Massacre at *Charlie Hebdo*." Or "Massacre on January 7."

On the seventh of each month, I shudder at the thought of hearing those words. January 7, 2015, will, of course, be a day marked with the seal of terror in the history of France. To me, it will remain the date when Georges died because of the most extreme violence. The cruelty of separation. The destruction of life. The unimaginable and the horrific fill me. There is also the fear of Georges's fear. Fear of his suffering. Like François Cavanna, Georges hated death.* He feared it, rejected it. I pointed out to him that he lacked humility. "*Stop crève*" ("Stop death"), Cavanna wrote. He wanted to believe in immortality and remained convinced that someday scientists would discover how to make us immortal. Georges smiled at

---

* François Cavanna (1923–2014) was an author and editor of satirical news-papers. He contributed to the creation and success of *Hara-Kiri* and *Charlie Hebdo*. He also translated books about famous cartoonists.

his words. He did not wish to be eternal, but he also couldn't live with the idea of death.

———

The central police station on the quai des Orfèvres, the third day after the attack. I climb the large staircase that leads to the office of the police captain in charge of the *Charlie Hebdo* case. Many police officers, both men and women, go up and down the stairs, pass by each other, in the chaos caused by the crisis. Words are called out: "This time, we've got them!" Got who? I can't understand, because I have no idea what has happened since January 7 at 1:15. My mind is fixed on Georges's body, his body I cannot find, despite the numerous calls made to the crisis unit on Wednesday and Thursday . . . Not one official could answer my question. Two days without knowing where Georges was laid to rest. Day and night, I thought only of his body, his face, his eyes, his lips that would never again kiss mine, his body abandoned somewhere, shot through with bullets, an autopsy performed, without my knowing a thing. The cruelty of silence.

I have difficulty climbing the stairs, for fear of the details I will be told and which I'd rather not know. Sitting in the police captain's office, I learn that two bullets went through

Georges's thorax. The officer undoubtedly did not have the entire autopsy report, or he was confusing it with another case. Because there were four bullets, as I would later learn from my lawyer. The first one hit the aorta. He died immediately.

At this moment, I imagined two holes in his chest. Two red holes, as in the poem "Le Dormeur du val" ("The Sleeper in the Valley"), which has stuck in my memory since my youth. The lines by Rimbaud surged up as I listened, dumbstruck, to the police captain. A young lieutenant was typing my replies to the questions being asked on an old computer. Had Georges talked to me about threats that he might have received in the mail? Was he afraid to go to work?

What could I say? That he had recently seemed worried, sometimes in distress? Could he sense the danger? Had he hidden the fact that he'd received threats, to protect me? He never talked to me about the fatwa against Charb, and the information had escaped me, strangely enough, even though I read the newspapers avidly. And we rarely discussed what was happening at *Charlie Hebdo*. I was aware only of the paper's financial problems. Was that what was worrying him, or did he have a premonition that something terrible was going to happen and found it difficult to hide that from me? "What's wrong?" I'd asked him several times in the weeks before the attack. "I worry about you . . ." he'd replied. "When I'm no longer here . . ." "But why think about the end of your life? You're in good health, you have projects you're passionate about. And life will go on as long as we love each other." He'd nodded. "I've been too careless in truth, and I love you, but I haven't protected you as I might have wished. I think about that often."

The police captain was still questioning me when Arnauld, my daughter's husband, came in, accompanied by one of my best friends, who was also a police captain. She held me tightly in her arms, which caused a flood of tears I could not hold back. After saying hello to them, the captain stood up and left the office. He came back a few minutes later holding Georges's briefcase, which I immediately recognized. I had given it to him the previous Christmas. The captain gave it back to me, coldly, for that is his job, then Georges's watch, which had recently been repaired, the gold chain I'd given him for his birthday, and his datebook. It had been found and examined, undoubtedly by the Anticrime Squad. I opened it to January 7. The day before, Georges had drawn an *X* through Tuesday the sixth, something he'd been doing regularly for a few years. "Why do you do that," I'd asked him, "as if you were counting the days?" A strange way of counting things that I'd never understood. Missing was the pen that matched the datebook, which I had given him for our silver wedding anniversary, some twenty years earlier. "We didn't find a pen with the datebook," the police captain told me. Finally, he gave me Georges's wallet, but his identity card was missing. I pointed that out. "We keep the identity cards," the captain explained. All that was left was his press card and some money. Arnauld had taken the briefcase from me.

My friend was talking to the captain about the repercussions of the attack. I held Georges's things tightly in my hands, as if they were treasures that had been lost, then found. The captain opened a drawer and took something out; I couldn't see what it was right away. Then he went around to the other side of the table piled high with files, came over to me, and handed me Georges's wedding ring. The tears I had managed to control for a few minutes started flowing again. He had worn that wedding ring since July 3, 1971; he'd never once taken it off since the day we got married in Canapville, a village in Normandy where we had commandeered two witnesses. The mayor was over an hour late. His Citroën had broken down. Georges liked reminding me that he had never taken off his ring, and that he was proud of that, because I had already lost two wedding rings, since I can't stand wearing any jewelry when I'm working. "A wedding ring is not jewelry." I can hear him saying those words, a loving reproach.

Two red holes while he was still holding his pencil.

8

THE SHOCK WAVE spread all over the world. Journalists called from England, the United States, Germany, Norway, and Italy, where Georges counted many famous cartoonists among his friends. One day, alone in a studio, I tell the BBC journalist who is interviewing me from London about the Post-its that now cover the walls of the apartment. Georges used to leave them for me on the table in the entrance hall if we weren't going out together, and especially on Tuesday nights when I was often out without him. "But what on earth could he write to you?" the young woman asked. "Simple words, but words of love." I'd gotten into the habit of keeping them in my desk drawer, but one day, I put some of them on the wall of the hallway that led to the kitchen. When my women friends came over, they were envious. They'd never gotten that kind of attention from their husbands or partners. After the attack, I covered all the walls of the apartment with the pink, yellow, and white Post-its. Every day, I stop in front of one and read it. I now know each message by heart and can recite them to myself. I see Georges's hand as he writes them. His hand was his work tool, and it was grazed by a stray bullet.

The day after the BBC broadcast, the journalist calls me back. Touched by what they've heard, her listeners want to see the Post-its on the Internet. I agree to allowing a photographer come to immortalize them. As soon as they appear on the BBC website, they are retransmitted throughout the media. They make their way around the world.

Beyond the emotion and astonishment of an entire people, the shock wave brought about a movement of brotherhood on January 11. *Brotherhood*, an outdated word that the January 7 attack had brought back into fashion. After what the French historian Pierre Nora called "a monstrous event" in the revue he founded, *Le Débat*, France stood in solidarity against the terrorists and acted. But which France? Points of view diverge.

———

To me, the essential thing was the number of people: four million took to the streets throughout the entire country, marching in close-knit rows, singing the "Marseillaise," assuring the police of their support as they passed by. A true union of people as no one had seen in a very long time. Some compared it to Victor Hugo's death in 1885, when a million people turned out to follow the funeral cortege in a great show of national unity.

But the shock wave went beyond France's borders, making it a global demonstration, from Japan to Africa to the United States. An enormous demonstration in favor of freedom of speech, undoubtedly, but also a reaction to the climate of war established by Muslim fundamentalists. A climate that was of concern to Pope Francis when he visited Sarajevo in June 2015. There he spoke of a "third world war" that was happening in small stages, and he encouraged a dialogue between cultures and religions. "Without which," he added, "barbarism and the cries of hateful fanatics will win out." And Pierre Nora in *Le Débat* explained that in this world movement, it was really France who had been supported, "the France of reason, of culture, of enlightenment, against the deadly obscurantism that claimed to come from Allah."

Even though everyone requested that I take part, I did

not participate in that movement. The Charlies went on the march, each wearing a headband with the name of the newspaper on it. But I had been overwhelmed by a state of shock that made it impossible for me to communicate in any way, in any way whatsoever. I only just managed to bear friends who wanted to be with me in my apartment, to distract me, in the positive sense of the word, from the tragedy that had struck my life. I found their laughter and chatter unbearable. I had the feeling that they were stealing my mourning, leading me away from my sadness. But I wanted to enclose myself in those very feelings because it gave me the illusion of still being with Georges a little, of prolonging my life with him.

———

And yet, when some of them came back from the demonstration on the evening of January 11, I asked them many questions. Who had marched? Young people? Older people too? Secular people? Catholics? Muslims? "There couldn't have been a lot of Muslims," a close friend told me. "In any case, I didn't see anyone from North Africa, Muslim or not."

The surviving Charlies went back to work, despite being physically and psychologically battered. It was essential that humor, satire, and even blasphemy win out over barbarism.

We must never forget that France is the country of impertinence, and has been since Rabelais and Voltaire. When the next issue came out, the French again demonstrated their solidarity. Many of them knew nothing about the satirical newspaper; others did not like the humor in it, or humor at all, even attacking it on occasion, and yet, out of solidarity, millions of them went to reserve their copies of what was dubbed the "survivors issue" at their corner newsstand. Those first Wednesdays following the attack, people waited in line. For whom? Why? Among the victims of the Kouachi brothers were humorists familiar to the French, like Cabu and Georges. And those French men and women identified with those men who, on many occasions, taught them to see things from a different angle. The way Georges had converted me to laughter, sarcasm, humor—thanks to him, I became a better person; I learned tolerance and freedom.

9

CHARLIE HEBDO, which was dying before the attack, with its twelve thousand subscribers and some forty thousand sales a month, soon achieved astronomical sales figures. How is it possible to forget that its journalists and cartoonists would undoubtedly be unemployed today if the attack had not taken place? The sale of seven million copies of the famous survivors issue brought in some 10 million euros.

"A nightmare, those millions!" exclaimed the commentator Patrick Pelloux. Taking over the helm of the newspaper became an interesting project all the same. Who would take on the responsibility? Charb had left no heir as editor, just a partner: Riss. The debate over the future of the newspaper did not stop there. Even though the survivors did not give much away in the days following the attack, the wave of millions of euros earned thanks to the volume of sales after the attack upset many people. Tension grew between the stockholders—two people and a few of their relatives—and the members of the editorial team, who were concerned about creating a collective that was better informed and that agreed on decisions. It was a shame that despite the show of solidarity aroused by the attack (and by the fact that the newspaper became a symbol of freedom of expression), managing the capital should have generated so much conflict, first reported in the press and then all over the world. That summer, an agreed solution was finally found, arbitrated by the minister of culture. *Charlie Hebdo* became the first newspaper in the "Statut d'entreprise solidaire de presse," a French law passed on April 17, 2015, creating a new legal press status. The law makes it a requirement for a qualifying company to reinvest at least 70 percent of its annual profits back into the company. The two stockholders decided to do the same with the remaining 30 percent, refusing to take any dividends. Finally, if any stockholding was to be allowed at all, only those collaborating on *Charlie Hebdo* could buy shares in the newspaper. That is what was announced by Riss. Watch this space. And Riss added in an interview in *Le Monde*, "When we sold less, we were more at peace. Now everyone is watching us, so many people expect us to take on a certain role, and everything could happen all over again." What precisely? A new conflict? To avoid that, let the newspaper remain the true symbol of freedom of expression! When Denis Robert's film dedicated to François Cavanna came out, a moving film on the history of the newspaper, a journalist suggested writing an article about it in the paper, which the management turned down. Cavanna's name would never be mentioned in the newspaper; he felt he had been dispossessed, as the name *Charlie Hebdo* belonged to him. It would not be worthy of its/ his history.

Alongside the stupendous sales, donations increased. Google spent 250,000 euros, the Associated Press and Pluralism sent 200,000 euros, and over two hundred thousand individuals donated a total of more than 1 million euros through the intermediary of the Internet platform Jaidecharlie.fr. Other contributions followed, and today the paper holds a kitty of more than 4 million euros. From the first days of February onward, *Charlie Hebdo*'s editorial administrators, as well as Patrick Pelloux, appeared on TV and radio to explain that the contributions would be given to the families of the victims as soon as possible.

And, in fact, exactly one month after the attack, on February 7, *Charlie Hebdo*'s lawyers invited the families involved to a meeting. The intention was generous, the objective to help us "go through mourning."

There were many of us at that meeting, the Charlies having decided to include the families of the victims of the Hyper-casher attack (the murder of four Jewish people at a kosher supermarket two days after the *Charlie Hebdo* attack), as well as the families of the murdered policemen. I listened to one of *Charlie Hebdo*'s lawyers describe the newspaper's high sales figures and give us information about the cartoonists and journalists, both present and absent during the attack, who were traumatized, who were experiencing post-traumatic stress symptoms, and who were in therapy, all the time imagining what Georges would have thought of it all.

He would have undoubtedly settled for a restrained expression of irony. Especially when he learned that the publication, now set up in the offices of the left-wing newspaper *Libération*, had just taken on a director of communications: the most famous of all the "spin artists," the woman who got Dominique Strauss-Kahn out of the mess we all know about. "Why have they hired her?" I asked, astounded. She was not at all the kind of person Cavanna or Cabu or Georges would have liked. What was she doing in the anarchic world of *Char-*

lie Hebdo? She was called in as backup, I was told, to manage the excessive number of interviews. In fact, she came to *Charlie* through one of Dominique Strauss-Kahn's advisers, Richard Malka, who was one of *Charlie Hebdo*'s lawyers. Was this the prelude to setting up a new team, called in to take over the reins of a newspaper whose business was booming? Rumors spread, but as we all know, you should never trust rumors.

After giving us the sales figures, one of the lawyers introduced us to the "pool of colleagues" whom we would need to help us face the procedures required by the Fonds de Garantie (the insurance company) to receive compensation or royalties, and whom we would need to work with if we decided to bring a civil case. Their fees would be paid by the newspaper, we were told. I appreciated the generosity that had been the source of that decision. In fact, putting together a claim for compensation required detailed knowledge of how to complete the insurance company's forms, before the Fonds de Garantie—an organization composed of experts and lawyers, as well as administrators appointed by the government—began examining them and starting the claims procedures. Then the lawyer moved on to the subject of gifts to the families. How should the distribution be organized? Would the beneficiaries be only the families of the victims of the newspaper, or should the families of the victims of the kosher supermarket and the policemen be included? The lawyer concluded that they were going to consider the matter.

The meeting continued. A psychiatrist, who was also a legal expert, explained that she would be at our disposal. "Going through mourning" was not an easy thing, especially after an attack, she explained. The consequences of the tragedy we had just lived through threatened to leave side effects that were best treated immediately. In any case, for the file to be sent to the insurance company, we were required to include a statement on our psychological condition, a kind of test to evaluate our suffering. This legal expert, who was young and charming, made you feel like going to see her—and even to agree to take the test, a test that, frankly, I found shocking. But she immediately warned us that she would be handing over our files to her colleagues.

After the meeting, I met a friend for lunch. We spent our time together wondering how to quantify suffering. Later on, I put the question to another friend, a distinguished psychoanalyst, who told me that the test had been designed in the United States, after the September 11 attacks, and that France had used it to evaluate moral prejudices after disasters and terrorist attacks in the past. This was surely not the best thing that France had borrowed from the United States, and my psychoanalyst friend was, to be honest, particularly shocked that I would have to undergo that type of ordeal.

Going through mourning. That was an expression Georges couldn't stand. He said that it didn't mean anything. We often discussed it without really agreeing. Georges rejected any psychiatric or psychoanalytical work. What was he afraid of? To look deep inside himself, in his inner temple, where you discover the truth about yourself and all the little compromises you make with yourself?

———

In the days that followed January 7, I felt nothing but pain and despair. Then the pain gave way to a kind of denial. From that point on, I irrationally maintained that I would live as if Georges were away on a trip. I added, quietly, as if to better convince myself, "Except Georges won't be coming back." But I said it without really wanting to believe it. In his room, I re-made the bed, tidied up the books scattered over the floor and the stacks of shirts and sweaters in his closet. I hung up ties that he'd never worn, except for the one he'd bought in a museum in Washington that was decorated with books. He often wore it for the launch of the Paris Book Fair. I spent time in the middle of his world. I sat at his desk and looked at each object that cluttered up the table. I put everything in order. I behaved as if he were away for a few days, and imagined him coming home. Three months after the attack, I still felt as if I would never emerge from this pretense.

The first time I had to go to the supermarket, I stood at the entrance to the store for a good ten minutes without knowing what I should buy. At that moment, I realized that until January 7, my shopping list contained things that Georges liked. I cooked food that he liked. And what about what I liked? Whatever that might have been, I didn't want anything; I walked up and down the aisles, overcome by nausea. I could picture Georges again, coming home with his mushrooms or baby artichokes, then settling down in the kitchen to prepare a delicious artichoke stew or, when they were in season, a pan of divine fried mushrooms. Now shopping is a chore I avoid as much as possible.

Procrastinating is one of the most terrible words in the world to me. And the day when I became aware I was procrastinating somewhat, curled up in moments of a past that made me languid and led me to feel numb and locked up, I rebelled against myself. I was not keeping the wonderful promises of those early days, when I had sworn I would shed no tears, that they would be dried by action. It was more than time to react, to confront the bureaucracy of the authorities, to put in order an estate that had been made difficult because of Georges's thousands of drawings and hundreds of publications, to transform all the work he had accomplished for more than fifty years into a respected body of work that was accessible to the greatest number of people.

One sunny day in spring in Briançon, opposite mountains still covered in snow, I found myself standing behind a rostrum that had been set up in the courtyard of the lycée where Georges had studied for a while, and where a great homage was being paid to him. Improvising a speech on the young man from Tunisia who had been left all alone and had disembarked, in awe, right in the middle of this snowy Briançon landscape, I spoke of how much his vitality, his vitality of spirit, and his very obvious wounds, which had always remained raw, had been the source of our emotional and intellectual life as a couple. That affirmation transformed me back into the person I had been before the January 7 attacks, the person who had to be reborn. My sadness would remain infinite, it would be a part of me from then on, but it would not prevent me from living.

10

DENIAL WAS REPLACED by anger and revolt. I had come to know a new land, the land of misery and solitude, and I had to understand why and use all my strength to fight it.

During the day, I made an effort to understand, and in detail, questioning the police, the minister of the interior, the "people involved," and the authorities, leafing through files, rereading articles, watching videos, listening to live programs, then listening again, examining everything that might have allowed the attack to be prevented. I wanted my simple happiness beside Georges to remain, our love, our plans, our discussions, our desires and their realization, all to remain, until life decided otherwise.

Threatened more than ever, as Angélique, the newspaper's

receptionist who took the phone calls and heard the insults, revealed, *Charlie Hebdo* still was not protected. As Thomas the actor pointed out, the police van had disappeared in November 2014. Charb had only two bodyguards instead of the original three. Why? And then I started to wonder: How could this attack have taken place right in the middle of Paris, in the offices of a satirical newspaper that received so many threats every day? Angélique spoke in front of the cameras of the Premières Lignes agency to explain that male voices had warned her they would actually cut off her head one day. Yet no additional measures seem to have been taken to protect Angélique and the others—the administrators, journalists, and illustrators. And among them, Georges. Four years before, a bomb had damaged the newspaper's offices. No one could ignore the fact that the newspaper was in real danger. So who had made the decision to lower the level of protection, and why?

I spent entire nights asking myself that question. When I finally fell asleep, the nightmares returned, carrying me into the darkness, a place from which I had the impression I would never escape. I would wake up with a start, thinking that I really needed to talk to Georges about it.

Those last months, we had never spoken about the threats against *Charlie Hebdo*.

"Darling, I'm going to *Charlie*." From now on, I will have to understand alone why, a few days after he said those words to me, I found myself at the morgue to identify his body. In the room in the mortuary where a psychologist greets you with a smile, I waited for them to prepare his remains. The night before the appointment, I had dreamed that, as in the movies, they would open a drawer that my husband was in. I woke up in such terror that I didn't think I would go.

The psychologist first led me behind a pane of glass. On the other side, Georges's body was resting on a rather high stand. A large white sheet covered his body. Only his face was visible. Not for a second did I think about what was under that sheet: a body shot through by bullets from a Kalashnikov. I was simply sorry I couldn't see his hands, couldn't take them in mine. I thought he looked good, handsome, and I recognized the irony in his smile. Not for a second did I imagine they had put makeup on him to cover the contusions; like the other cartoonists, he'd fallen facedown onto the ground. Once next to him, I stroked his face, then his lips, then I kissed him. He looked twenty years younger. I didn't want to ever leave him. I felt calm, next to him.

When I arrived, the psychologist said that she had rarely seen a dead person with such a serene face. "I didn't know

Monsieur Wolinski," she added, "because I don't read the papers or watch television, but when I saw him, I was surprised by the tranquility I could read on his face." Listening to this person, full of sweetness and compassion, I imagined that Georges must not have suffered. That he fell after being shot without really understanding what was happening to him. And that was so like him.

———

I continued stroking his cheek and kissing him, as if he were taking a nap on the living room sofa. As soon as he'd finished a cartoon, he would happily stretch out, holding *Le Monde*, and fall asleep. Not that he was bored reading *Le Monde*, but as soon as he closed his eyes, he fell asleep. Lucky or unlucky? He spent many hours sleeping, in order to be rejuvenated, he would say, to have several days all in one day. And several lives in his one life. In the morgue, I wanted to take a picture of him, to keep this final image of him forever. The psychologist advised against it. Feeling so emotional, I didn't ask her why. Today I regret it. That picture may have saved me some time.

The young psychologist soon made me aware that I had to go. Families of the other victims were waiting outside. I looked at Georges one last time. It was no longer the Georges I had held; it was Georges's body.

The same idea occurred to me the morning he was placed in the coffin. I kissed him once again, fully aware that his lips were not the same as the ones Georges had used to kiss me when we'd gotten married forty-seven years earlier at the town hall in Canapville. Afterward, he had taken me to a field where we had made love all afternoon before falling asleep beneath the stars. You couldn't imagine a more wonderful wedding night. It was his gift to me. Then, left-winger that he was, he took me on a long trek through the countries of the Eastern Bloc. We met with bitter illustrators who envied his great freedom. He introduced me to them as his "blond little girl."

For a long time, he wanted me to remain that innocent woman who, like a doll, gave in to his least desire. But the doll was hatching a feminist, rebellious by nature. Later on, when we felt nostalgia for our youth, he would return to the blond little girl he'd met in the editorial office of the *Journal du Dimanche*, and he'd tell me he missed the days when he could "play" with me. Beneath the feminist left-winger lay an eternal male chauvinist.

But on January 7, the blond little girl disappeared amid the rubble of the massacre.

11

GETTING UP EVERY morning is difficult. I feel like a soldier who must hurry to be at the appointed place for the next battle. Which battle? I don't know. But almost every day, some opportunity presents itself. And the soldier must respond to the duty calling her and find the strength to act once more.

But I don't really have any strength. And in the end, I wind up inventing my battles. I make appointment after appointment to fill the endless desert of my days. I spend more time on the phone than I should. I put the radio on very loud because I want someone to talk to me. I listen to writers; first Annie Ernaux, then, later on, Simone de Beauvoir. I have the impression they are speaking to me and not to the journalist who is interviewing them. In the evening, I accept invitations, to avoid being alone as the day ends, sitting in front of a meal that I can't manage to finish. Then comes the time to go to bed, the decisive moment. I take more tranquilizers to try to avoid nightmares, but still they wake me up with a start, so I spend my sleepless nights going through thousands of photos of Georges. I have the impression of being engulfed in a war that has become internalized. The goal of the terrorists who murdered Georges and his friends was to spread terror. I would like to contribute to fighting against terror, but it remains deeply rooted within me. This is what is really at stake: to rid yourself of terror. And so I continue my quest, try to understand, to explain. Is someone, somewhere, guilty? I question, listen, read.

In the past, Georges used to mock me, saying, "You always look for someone who is guilty, in everything." He was right. But the generalized "clear conscience" that followed the attack did not satisfy me. Where could I get answers to my questions? From the police? At *Charlie Hebdo*? And how would I rebuild my own life? By murdering Georges, the terrorists tore out a part of me. Before being able to reconstruct my life, I had to reclaim that part of myself.

So, the police?

In April 2013, two years after the fire in the *Charlie Hebdo* offices, the major police union, Alliance Police Nationale, had already pressured the government to cut down the surveillance of *Charlie Hebdo*. How could they dedicate so many resources to protecting a newspaper that spit on everything and everyone, starting with the police force? Members of the union had distributed leaflets revealing that on April 4, during a meeting with the director of the DOPC, the agency responsible for maintaining public order, representatives from the union had "demanded the immediate cessation of the *Charlie Hebdo* assignment." For more than seven months, they complained, "the DOPC task force had been providing as many as nine officers a day to protect the private offices of a newspaper." To the union, the police were not "security guards." They were responsible, above all, to carry out state assignments. In the same leaflet, they continued: "Is the DOPC so rich in numbers that it can afford this luxury?" Whatever the case may be, their numbers were clearly insufficient given the situation.

To the union, providing surveillance for *Charlie Hebdo*, whose offices had just been destroyed by a firebomb and which continually received threats, was a luxury during this period of shortage of police officers on the ground. Did the authorities finally give in to the pressure? In July 2014, Jean-Jacques Urvoas, the president of the Senate Judicial Committee, pointed out during a session of the Assemblée nationale that antiterrorist specialists periodically warned of an imminent threat.* On October 1, 2014, when *Charlie Hebdo* was already in its new offices on rue Nicolas-Appert, after publishing an issue that once again had a cover showing a caricature of the Prophet Mohammed, the director of the prefect of police, Laurent Nuñez, reinstated the "static" protection: a police van and officers who would do shifts at the front door of the building. A little while later, moreover, he explained in *Le Monde*, "the illustrator, Charb, would call us when he was publishing a risky issue and we reinstated the static protection."

But under union pressure, police officials removed that regular protection a few days later and replaced it with a type of surveillance called "active": patrols that went by the offices almost every thirty minutes. And yet, according to police sources, the threats against Charb continued to intensify, which Angélique, the newspaper's receptionist, confirmed—and which was contrary to what Gérard Biard, one of the newspaper's contributors, stated when the attack took place, saying that "the threats had seemed less serious."

---

*The Assemblée nationale is the lower house of the French parliament.

Gérard Biard and Angélique must not have spoken to each other, or perhaps the newspaper's contributors preferred to turn a blind eye. "We didn't want to live in a bunker," Patrick Pelloux stated after the attack. But now that ten of their colleagues have been murdered, they are actually forced to work in a place with intense security, with, for some of them, police protection twenty-four hours a day.

Measures taken too late. Especially given that Loïc Garnier, the director of the antiterrorist coordination unit, stated in September 2014, three months before the attack—as had Jean-Jacques Urvoas in the Assemblée nationale—that "the question was no longer if there would be an attack in France, but when." And Franck Brinsolaro, Charb's bodyguard, who was experienced in dangerous situations after having taken on numerous missions that were particularly perilous, notably in Afghanistan, confided to his wife that "he could sense a catastrophe was about to happen." So danger truly was present.

It is unimaginable that Franck Brinsolaro, who didn't even have time to draw his weapon on the day of the attack, did not pass on his fears to his superiors. But there was a negative atmosphere in the Protection Unit he belonged to. During 2014, the press echoed this, after the suicide of two police officers, one of whom had been in charge of security for Bernadette Chirac. The officers in the Protection Service certainly were filled with discontent because their workload was becoming heavier and heavier. According to union representatives, this was due to a growing number of protections dubbed "bogus protections," which had often been arranged without the prior agreement of the antiterrorist unit, which was a procedural prerequisite. This way of doing things had been denounced in the press. Think of the Saudi prince who had asked for, and received, protection to go shopping on the French Riviera . . .

This is why the police surveillance van had disappeared in front of the building at 10, rue Nicolas-Appert, providing an unusual window of opportunity for the terrorists to attack. According to a police source, the minister of the interior, when questioned, is said to have replied that surveillance of that type would have caused even more deaths. Why? Because of the lack of training of the police force, apart from the antiterrorist unit, the GIGN, and the BRI.* Everyone confirms this and complains about it. They feel powerless in the face of terrorists and their heavy weaponry. Armed with their SIG

---

*The Brigade de recherche et d'intervention (BRI) is the French Research and Intervention Brigade.

Sauger semiautomatics, they don't think they have a chance against the Kalashnikovs the jihadists use. And the jihadists, as we saw only too well during the January 7 attack, act in greater cold blood, because they have been excellently trained for months—in Yemen or elsewhere.

Only three days a year are dedicated to training a French police officer in the use of firearms—insufficient to turn them into crack snipers, fighters who could measure up to the challenge posed by jihadists. And another major problem is their bulletproof vests: the most effective one weighs twenty-two pounds! So many police officers wear a lighter one—which is totally useless against rounds from a Kalashnikov. And yet those were the vests that the bicycle patrolmen who first got the message saying shots had been heard in *Charlie Hebdo*'s building were wearing (even if they were unaware, remember, that *Charlie Hebdo* was in their area). The Kouachi brothers, on the other hand, wore heavier bulletproof vests, as can be seen in the videos.

As for the vehicles, many are inadequate. It was said that four million of them would be renovated throughout 2015. According to police sources, more than ten thousand had to be sent to the junkyard. A recent Alliance Police Nationale leaflet carried the headline "Police equals national monument in danger!"* In a drawing, a French policeman crumbles opposite a jihadist wearing a balaclava and brandishing a Kalashnikov.

What conclusion can we draw from all this? Today, despite the threats, ordinary police officers, who are not part of the GIGN, the antiterrorist unit, or the BRI, are not in any state to respond to the terrorist threat. And they all know it. After asking many questions, I realized that the GIGN, the antiterrorist unit, and the BRI are not sent out in response to simple telephone calls. But in January 2015, their men were brought in two days after the *Charlie Hebdo* attack, when the terrorist brothers were holed up in a printing factory in Dammartin-en-Goële, north of Paris.

In the aftermath of the *Charlie Hebdo* murders and the killings at the kosher supermarket, the French government decided to deploy ten thousand soldiers. Ten thousand men, a number unheard of since the Algerian War. Moreover, ac-

---

*This headline is a reference to a very popular French TV program from the 1960s with the same title, which looked at national historical buildings, monuments, etc., that were falling into disrepair. Volunteers were recruited to renovate the buildings, and the program showed the structures before and after.

cording to *Le Monde*, the Secretariat-General for National Defense and Security convinced the president of France to save 18,750 jobs out of the 34,000 that were supposed to be cut. In addition, discussions are going on to establish a system that would link the army, the police, and the gendarmerie.* Is the fight against terrorism finally beginning to get organized?

---

*The gendarmerie is a branch of the army that polices a specific local area outside Paris. The police, the army, and the gendarmerie have traditionally not easily cooperated with each other.

12

THE FIRST TIME I thought about Georges dying was well before the year 2000. We were on vacation in Corsica, the island
where Georges once told me that he wanted to be buried,
facing the sea. We spent our time swimming together in the
clear green waters of the Mediterranean. The first days, he
swam quickly, strongly. I lagged behind, never able to catch up.
One evening, after we'd gotten back to our hotel from a rather
boozy dinner where he'd had several whiskeys and smoked a
few cigars, I noticed that he was walking with difficulty. His
face was drawn and pale.

The next day, we went back to the beach. I watched him
dive in. I didn't see him come up out of the water. Worried, I
walked over to the shore and saw him swimming very slowly

back to the beach. Once back on the beach, he complained about a terrible pain in his left arm. He was having trouble breathing. "It's your heart," I said. "We have to go to the ER." "No, it's muscular," he claimed. "I must have hurt myself moving the beach umbrella the other night."

In the days that followed, he didn't swim; he just got in the water for a few minutes. I asked him why. Again the story about moving the beach umbrella. I arranged for us to go back to Paris early. He didn't really object. But once in Paris, he made an appointment with his physical therapist and refused to allow me to contact a cardiologist.

I remember that I was crossing the place de l'Assemblée Nationale when I got the doctor's call. Georges had been rushed to the hospital in Tenon. He'd had a heart attack. I hailed a taxi and went to the hospital. He was being taken care of by doctors and would be operated on the next day. I stayed with him, holding his hand and squeezing it tightly in mine and kissing him. The doctor who came in for his night shift was the only one who could make me leave Georges's room. I had the feeling I would never see him alive again. That night, I had one nightmare after the other. One of them woke me with a start: I could see Georges disappearing into the distance as I tried in vain to catch up to him. What would become of me without him? I was no longer Georges's wife who had been abandoned at the side of the road, but a little lost girl.

That image was still in my mind when I woke up. Until then, he had been a kind of Pygmalion to me—but a Pygmalion who had also taught me how to liberate myself. What would happen to me if he died? How could I go on living without his gaze? When I got to the hospital the day of the operation, I thought again about how fragile Georges's health was. But he would be unsinkable, I was convinced of that. Imagining his death was impossible for me.

Living without his gaze? The question has come back again and again since the attack. After the operation to give him stents, he came home feeling pretty well, and went to *Charlie Hebdo* the next day. This was still when Cavanna was respected, when his word counted for something. A time when Georges would become revitalized at *Charlie*, as he had at *Paris Match*, when Roger Thérond took over the magazine. When Philippe Val was running *Charlie Hebdo*, the climate changed: he claimed he would get its finances in order, proposing shares to new stockholders, which Georges didn't take part in because he refused, he wanted to turn the newspaper into a true publishing business. All sorts of arguments and divisions followed.

In 2008, in one of the columns he was so good at writing, and as boldly as ever, Siné attacked President Sarkozy's son Jean, who was about to marry the Jewish heiress Jessica Sebaoun-Darty.* In this type of matter, Siné pushed his freedom of expression—which was always borderline when it came to the Jews—to an extreme. Val, who was a friend of Carla Bruni-Sarkozy, immediately reacted by firing the cartoonist. The International League against Racism and Anti-Semitism (LICRA) filed a formal complaint against him, and various petitions followed, but a year later, Siné was nevertheless acquitted on the grounds of freedom of expression. He'd used his right to satirize. However, Val began to be seriously challenged. His "authoritarianism," which some reproached him for, upset the team of talented and eccentric artists. During an editorial meeting, Riss, the owner of the newspaper since the attack, became unable to stand Val's attitude, and grabbed his arm and prepared to throw him out a window. But Tignous rushed to save his friend. Such drama

---

* Maurice Sinet (1928–2016), known professionally as Siné, was a French political cartoonist known for his anti-Semitism and anarchism. Siné claimed that Jean Sarkozy was considering converting to Judaism for financial gain. He never did convert.

was not unusual at the heart of the editorial team. A few seconds later, everyone around the table was laughing again.

That same year, following an article published in *Le Monde*, the team, whose members received a very modest salary, learned that two years before, the newspaper had recorded a profit of nearly a million euros. In fact, the first cover that showed the Prophet Mohammed, illustrated by Cabu and with the caption "It's hard being loved by morons," had attracted five hundred thousand readers. In a situation such as that, Choron, the former editor in chief, used to give everyone a raise in a festive atmosphere with the champagne flowing. But the current shareholders preferred sharing the booty of dividends among themselves, in total secrecy. The cartoonists and journalists had to be content with their meager salaries. In such matters, however, the secret always comes out. And the team had a huge fight. Then, a year later, Val became the director of France Inter, and left the already sinking ship.* To pay for the shares he was giving up, the paper's owners found it necessary to sell the offices on the rue Étienne-Marcel that *Charlie* owned. That was the first departure. Val's depar-

---

*France Inter is a major public radio channel that is part of Radio France.

ture signaled the arrival of Charb, his "heir." The newspaper became more political, trying to find its niche faced with competition by the *Canard enchaîné*, which had always been very successful.* But the readers didn't follow. Not even the newspaper's staunchest supporters, such as the radical left.

One Wednesday, a little while before the attack, after one of the editorial meetings, Georges came home from the newspaper looking somber and annoyed. He explained that Charb had lectured him to stop drawing cartoons that didn't deal with current events. Current events meant, in particular, mocking the Prophet Mohammed and his followers, who were deemed dangerous, blinkered fanatics. Between the work he was doing for the *Journal du Dimanche* and *Paris Match*, Georges couldn't take any more politics. To him, *Charlie Hebdo* represented exactly the kind of release he needed at the time, a place where he could draw what was funny to him, more often dealing with social rather than political issues. That was what the satirical weekly newspaper where he'd started out meant to him: a place where taboos could be broken. In May 1977,

---

* *Le Canard enchaîné* is a well-established (1915) satirical weekly newspaper with headquarters in Paris. Its name translates as "the chained duck" or "the chained newspaper," as "*canard*" is French slang for "newspaper."

he wrote in one of his columns: "When I met the *Hara-Kiri* team, in the 1960s, politics was not discussed, as far as I remember. We shared only an extraordinary irreverence for institutions and taboos, which were numerous at the time. I have to say that, what with sex, religion, the army, advertising, work, family, and the country, there was plenty to satirize." Back then, the religion he mocked was Catholicism, the religion of the pope and the Catholic fundamentalists, which was both his and Cabu's favorite subject. People have forgotten that certain cartoons from the 1970s and '80s put the pope in the same irreverent situations as the Prophet Mohammad of today's cartoons. Sometimes there was a trial, but never a bomb.

In 2014, Charb's *Charlie Hebdo* did not make fun of the same things as in the 1970s, but always in the name of freedom of expression and in defense of secularism, the paper did not hesitate to outdo everyone else. Delfeil de Ton, one of the very first friends of *Hara-Kiri* from 1967 onward, and thus one of Georges's earliest colleagues, reported in the magazine *L'Observateur* that Georges once told him, "I think that we are reckless imbeciles who have taken a pointless risk. We think we are invulnerable. For dozens of years, we have been provoking, and one day that provocation will turn against us."

Was that why, especially after Cavanna's death, Georges

went to the newspaper less often, apart from a few Wednesdays each month? Charb also reproached him for that. In the difficult situation in which Georges found himself, Charb's thoughts were not well received. Georges was thinking about his professional future. He wanted to have more time to paint and write, while continuing to draw for the papers. That was the life he dreamed of at the time. Moreover, he had taken steps to get a studio where he would have more room to spread out his canvases and set up his easels. And he wouldn't have enough time for that if he spent entire days at *Charlie Hebdo* filling the pages of a newspaper whose coffers were empty, a newspaper that he felt might have no future. He, on the other hand, wanted to prepare himself for what would follow. And he was determined to do so.

13

FEBRUARY, A MONTH after the attack, the *Charlie* survivors visited their umpteenth new offices with good company: specialists in armor-plating and bombproof systems. From that point onward, they would be working in a bunker. Writing these lines, I recall what Patrick Pelloux said shortly after the attack, explaining on TV that "for the *Charlie* team, it wasn't possible to work in a bunker. They didn't talk about security."

So it took the murder of ten of them, Georges included, for them to stop working in a carefree way.

Actually, since the time they were located on the rue Étienne-Marcel, *Charlie Hebdo* had moved continuously. In April 2011, because of their difficult financial situation, the team moved to the porte de Montreuil. Barely one year later, feeling they were too far from the center of Paris, they started looking for new offices in the 20th arrondissement, on boulevard Davout. There the cartoonists didn't hesitate to hang their drawings in the windows. In November, when an issue of *Sharia Hebdo* came out after the elections in Tunisia (which voted in an Islamist party), there was an arson attack. Accommodated for a while by the left-wing newspaper *Libération*, the team was again forced to find new offices. They ended up on rue Serpollet, in the same arrondissement.

This time, it was under police surveillance: on the ground floor of the new building was a police station. Several police cars were permanently parked in front of the building. But as the newspaper lost more and more readers, the management team once again decided to find less expensive premises. The city of Paris then offered the paper space in a commercial building where the rent was very low, on the rue Nicolas-Appert, run by a property management company partially owned by the city. As the newspaper's financial situation had become so difficult, the team signed up. But the building had several entrances and doors were often left open, because the companies with offices throughout the building's three floors used messengers, as people who work there stated—people who also were attacked by the Kouachi brothers because they didn't know that the satirical paper was located there.

So, a building with no security. Nevertheless, it was soon decided that work had to be done to make the premises safer, and it began in the summer of 2014. For the authorities, the satirical paper remained a target. The security section of the local administration, which was authorized to work on this type of case, was brought in. An inspector was appointed, responsible for finding ways to make the offices safe. He soon got in touch with the paper's accountant, then met with him and his wife. The inspector immediately informed them that the building was seriously vulnerable in several areas. He particularly mentioned the access points on the two different streets, one on 6, allée Verte and the other on 10, rue Nicolas-Appert, which both led to the same building, as well as another access point in the basement, since the entrance to the parking lot provided passage from one road to the other. But the choice had been made, and it was too late to find somewhere else. Work would have to be done to make the place safe, and that was that.

Given the risks run by the paper, it was an unwise decision. The premises themselves were a problem. They were narrow and only had one exit door, which meant that the escape route could easily be blocked in an emergency. After his visit, the inspector left with everything he needed to carry out his study. He came back later to detail the security measures necessary, which mainly had to do with the offices.

That day, he was greeted by the accountant's wife, to whom he presented several possibilities regarding making the space safe for the newspaper, the cartoonists, and the journalists. First, in spite of the narrowness of the space, he advised the installation of two airlock doors, which had to be opened in sequence, like the ones in certain banks. But he immediately realized that this would never be done, as the *Charlie Hebdo* staff had already started moving in. His second proposal: transform the small waiting area, where the staff had planned to put desks for the webmaster and the receptionist, into a buffer zone to protect access to the editorial room and the rest of the newspaper. It would be an area whose walls were bulletproof, actually turning it into an armor-plated room, at the end of which the two doors leading to the editorial room and Charb's office would also be armor-plated and could be opened only by entering a code. Other measures included putting alarms in the offices with a videophone, installing a camera on the landing, and installing video cameras in the armor-plated waiting area. Finally, the inspector recommended putting special blinds on the windows that overlooked the street.

The report was passed on to the local government representative, who sent it to the newspaper's management team, reminding them that the cartoonists were in great danger. The inspector responsible for the report had, moreover, detailed the threats along with his security recommendations. He was then told: "We would never be hit, not us." Lack of foresight, carelessness, the feeling that humor makes people invulnerable? Finally, the paper's own management team decided that a simple video camera would be installed in the entrance.

"Could we force them to protect themselves against their will?" the inspector wondered aloud when I asked him if they couldn't have been obliged to accept the security measures. And he added that they could have asked for financial aid from the city of Paris, even the Ministry of Culture, which would have helped, given the attack on the paper a few years before. At the local government headquarters, and especially in the department that dealt with vulnerable targets, a commando attack with use of military weapons had even been envisaged—which was why the drastic security measures had been recommended. Even without the security doors, the Kouachis' bullets would not have penetrated an armor-plated door. And even if the brothers had decided to use grenades, the team would certainly have had time to react.

Yes, there were flaws in the security preparations at the *Charlie Hebdo* office, and they were numerous—because unlike the local government's department for vulnerable targets, the state, the police force, and the newspaper's management team refused to accept the idea that we were already at war. A war of ignorance against culture, against the freedom so cherished by Georges, against obscurantism.

Yes, Saïd and Chérif Kouachi certainly had a great window of opportunity. In the days preceding January 7, when Saïd was bored in Reims with nothing to do but pray, and Chérif and his accomplices in Asnières were planning the attack, they probably didn't expect that it would be so easy to carry out their massacre. In the end, they would find only one obstacle to getting in: the security code. Not difficult to surmount when you're armed with a Kalashnikov.

Did the General Directorate for Internal Security allow itself to be fooled by the tricks taught to the terrorists during their training in Yemen? Chérif Kouachi had been identified in 2011. He'd been training with Al-Qaida in the Arabian Peninsula and was instructed to keep a low profile, hide his fundamentalism, and shave off his beard once he returned to France. Alerted by the Americans that he was back, the French authorities put the Kouachi brothers under surveillance. But they were obeying al-Qaida's orders, and, as they seemed to have come around, were no longer considered a threat, so the surveillance stopped. They had become "sleeper agents." This is why, three days after the attack, the US Department of Homeland Security held a press conference to inform the reporters that "nothing in the surveillance of the Kouachis or Coulibaly led us to believe that they were preparing an attack."*

———

Five thousand radicalized people are listed in the *S* file (*S* for state security). The files are reviewed every two years, and if the people in them have not been reported for any incidents, their names are removed. How many sleeper agents are there in our country? Since the publication of the caricatures of Moham-med, al-Qaida's leaders have been determined to act against Western countries, and particularly against France. Hence the announcement of the 2013 fatwa against Charb, which was published in the magazine *Inspire*, founded by al-Qaida.

The Worst Is Yet to Come—that was the prophetic title of one of Georges's books.

———

* Amedy Coulibaly was the terrorist who killed a policeman on January 8, 2015, and four people in a kosher supermarket on January 9.

14

SIX MONTHS LATER.

Tonight, as with every night, I walk through Georges's office, which remains just as he left it, an unfinished sketch on the drawing board, a lead pencil and an eraser next to it, his black leather vest on the chair, three felt pens in its pocket, his wobbly stack of daily newspapers on his desk. I walk over to the bookcase to replace a book. Suddenly I realize that the day I move, everything will be dismantled: the drawing board, the table bought at the flea market in Saint-Ouen, and, of course, his collection of books on press drawings, paintings, and artists' biographies—a collection that he started more than fifty years ago.

Often, if he had run out of ideas, I would see him dive

into one of those books or his own archives to get inspiration that the daily press didn't provide for him. Right at the top of the bookcase, he had arranged Cavanna's many publications. I pulled out one of them, *Coeur d'artichaut* (*Artichoke Heart*), which I'd read when it first came out. The dedication made me smile: "To get to an artichoke heart, Maryse, you have to pull off its leaves, Maryse, like a Daisy. But when it's done, the heart is left and that's the best part." I put the book back in its place. Then I sat down in Georges's armchair, where he'd spent many long days, and let the tears flow, tears I had held back for so long.

I stood up, eyes still fixed on the bookcase, and swore to myself that nothing would be dismantled. That was how I got the idea to donate the office-workshop to the International Center for Caricatures, Press Drawings, and Humor in Saint-Just-le-Martel, a center that was opened thanks to a report Georges wrote with a curator from the Bibliothèque nationale at the request of President Chirac. The very next day, I called Gérard Vanderbroucke, the director of the museum and an elected official from the region. I didn't tell him about my idea, I simply asked him to come and see me the next time he was visiting Paris. Which he did. When I explained my idea to him, he was very moved. A week later, he came back with several friends of the museum who had known Georges well; every year, he had taken part in a festival of drawings in Saint-Just-le-Martel. They took photos of the office-studio, noting the slightest detail so they could reconstruct the room exactly. I have conserved those photos, which are so precious to me; they remind me of the time when Georges would sit at his table, early in the morning, surrounded by his newspapers and magazines. Holding a pencil, he would underline, circle, cut out, and archive articles until he found the idea that would inspire his drawing. In the afternoon, after a nap, he would sit down at his drawing board and finish the morning's sketch.

On July 8, about a dozen friends of the museum accompanied Gérard Vanderbroucke to dismantle the brightly lit room that Georges had abandoned because the terrorists took his life.

"Darling, I'm going to *Charlie*." When I woke up, I asked myself how I was going to bear letting the drawing board leave my apartment. I convinced myself that it was an excellent idea and that, from time to time, I could go and visit it in the little town near Limoges where Georges had tried to convince me to go with him so many times. My children and friends also thought that donating the office to a museum was a very good idea. Now I had to go through with it, stay strong all day long, not allow myself to shed a single tear, prevent any weakness, comfort myself through taking action so as not to give in to despair.

The atmosphere among the movers was joyful. Everyone did his part. Some took charge of the furniture and some organized the books and other things in numbered cardboard boxes, so that when they arrived, every book, every object, would be in the right place. They spent some time deciding how to dismantle the drawing board. I didn't know where Georges had put the instructions, and it was pointless to look for them in his files, whose contents never matched the file's name. For an instant, I wished they wouldn't be able to do it. If I turned it over and laid it flat, I could surely use it as a writing table . . .

They managed to fold it up and take it downstairs. I went out onto the balcony; from there, I watched it go into the truck. Suddenly I remembered that David André, the film-maker who had made a movie about January 7 and who absolutely wanted to film the moving of the office, hadn't arrived yet. And the table was no longer there!

I phoned him, and as he said he was on our street, we decided to take the drawing board out of the back of the truck. The friends of the museum very kindly agreed to put it back together on the sidewalk while the cameraman got ready to film. For the few minutes needed for the take, it was the main attraction in the neighborhood. I watched the scene from the balcony. Passersby huddled against storefront windows to see the extraordinary filming of a drawing board sitting on a Parisian sidewalk. Then they loaded it back into the truck. I saw it for the last time. I remembered the day when Georges had come back from the United States with the drawing board under his arm and kissed me when I opened the door for him, then carried me across the apartment to his bedroom. There will never be such happy moments anymore.

15

DURING THIS SUMMER, which I am spending alone in Paris, I often find myself rereading the Post-its that Georges left me. I walk down the long hallway where I have lined them up and look at them. I still think of Georges's hand scribbling them, and I always will. I recall the tenderness contained in his words, in his gestures. The same tenderness that frightened him so much when he was about to turn fifty.

One evening in August, I turned on the radio while eating dinner and heard his voice on France Culture. At first, I was so surprised that I hardly recognized it. I listened, very moved. He was telling an anecdote from when François Mitterrand was campaigning in the 1981 election. We were invited to take the bus to Lille, where the future president of France was going to give one of his important speeches. When it was over, Georges went to join his friends who were heading for the buffet table. Mitterrand, who had come down from the rostrum and was looking for a glass of wine, noticed Georges, the cartoonist who was very irreverent toward anything to do with Mitterrand, in spite of Georges's leftist leanings. From a distance, I saw them talking and laughing. So I decided to join them. Georges put his arm around me and introduced me. "I already know you," Mitterrand said. "I see you every week in Wolinski's drawings." I smiled, not very comfortable at the remark, which made me Georges's muse. And yet, I can't deny it: I was his muse for forty-seven years. A muse who was loving and rebellious, both at the same time. I won't ever deny it. They were the most wonderful years of my life.

In the silence of the apartment, I told myself that perhaps, soon, I might give myself permission to think about what my life was going to be like. The life I had to rebuild. Did I have the means to do it? Faced with pain, sometimes denial, often with the need to act, I felt that I had not taken the time to go through a period of mourning. And I always came back to the same question: What exactly does that mean, to go through a period of mourning? Perhaps it was what I had been doing for six months, moving from shock to isolation, to extreme agitation and a feeling of abandonment, from denial to anger . . .

Today I am moving into a space where changes are taking place; I'm facing the future, that theater of the unknown, which causes fragility and a feeling of instability. Months have passed, and I no longer resist time, which puts distance between that Wednesday when Georges left for *Charlie Hebdo* and the autumn that will lead me to my first year without him. A year without him, how is that possible? Without his gaze, his caresses, his admiration, his loving words, both spoken and written? After having held on to him for so long, having so desired to hold him in my arms, so wished for him to guide me through life, I let him go. I let him take flight. I no longer write "darling Georges" in my datebook when we are to meet. The last meeting won't take place; we will never live on the quayside. But before making an important decision, I still can't help thinking: What would Georges say? Would he approve?

To live or to die? Allow Georges to take his place in the picture frames that surround me, serious photos, funny photos? I remember saying to him, shortly after my mother died, "When you die, you're nothing more than a photo in a picture frame." He'd smiled.

In my office, on the mantelpiece of the fireplace, I put a photo of him in a ski outfit about to start a competition. He must have been sixteen years old. I love that photo, which I recently discovered. He's there, he's looking at me. When I have dinner alone, in the kitchen, I sit facing a shelf on which, until January 7, sat all sorts of jars and teapots, as well as a plate painted by him showing me naked, in front of a window, staring at the moon. I remember that summer in the Lubéron. With his potter friend, he decided to make something in the workshop. A cricket, who was quite ill, landed on one of the tables and died a few seconds later. Tony, the potter, chose to make a cast of it. Georges and I decided that Tony should create a dinner service for us that would have that cricket on each piece. When I set the table and hold one of those plates with the cricket and see that it is beginning to fade, I relive that moment and my eyes fill with tears.

Near the plate, on the shelf, I put a framed photo of him in which he is posing, smiling: the smile of a happy man. I have dinner looking at it and smile to myself. I think of the loving words he said to speak of the happiness I brought him. I am proud that I had, sometimes, pulled him out of his pathological melancholy.

Dahhling,
Tonight, I forgot everything, the drawing, Anne G's
party, the only thing I didn't forget was you. I love
you, G.

I can't wait to join you in the Lubéron. I've loved you
for 42 years now, G.

Sometimes, when the days are too difficult, I want to shout out to him that life without him is hell, a hell I will never escape, that my future is a desert, that he should stop smiling in that photo. Or that he should come out of that picture frame, as in the Woody Allen film we liked so much, *The Purple Rose of Cairo*. Like Cecilia, its heroine, I want Georges to come out of the picture frame as Tom Baxter did, so he can lead me to new loving adventures, holding a pencil, drawing the curves of my hips on the pages of the sketchbook that is always in his pocket.

I know. I have to stop dreaming, I mustn't give in to the temptation of denial. Today I must be led by my own gaze. It has not been simple to accept that idea, and let Georges take flight.

But for him, from now on, I must go forward.

Acknowledgments

I would first like to thank my editors: Olivier Bétourné, the president of Éditions du Seuil, for having trusted me, and Frédéric Mora, for having supported my need to write what my life has been like since the attack.

I also thank Luc Hermann, codirector of the Premières Lignes agency, whose offices were on the same floor as *Charlie Hebdo*, and who was the first to guide me and allowed me to meet the journalists from his agency, who were all so kind that I can never forget them.

I thank my faithful friend Patrice Trapier, deputy director of the *Journal du Dimanche*, who gave me access to his contacts.

I thank everyone whom I didn't have to call on but who spontaneously contacted me to help clarify certain questions, especially the police officers, whose anonymity I insist on respecting. Everyone gave me the strength to continue to write, to continue to live.

I thank Chantal Schmeltz, who, despite being so traumatized, told me what happened to her and the chaos that reigned in the building at 10, rue Nicolas-Appert that January 7.

I thank the Comédie Bastille, and in particular Thomas Joussier and Nathalie Rolandez, who had spent some time in the theater and directly experienced the events of January 7, opening the theater's doors to the survivors and the families of the victims.

I thank the people from *Charlie*, among them the survivors, who told me what they lived through when the massacre took place, as well as Véronique Portheault and Patrick Pelloux, who accompanied me when I visited the newspaper's offices, after the seals were removed.

Finally, I would like to thank my companions in pain: my daughter, Elsa; Chloé Verlhac, Tignous's wife; and Hélène Honoré, Honoré's daughter; as well as Arnauld Champremier-Trigano, my son-in-law. Everyone helped me move forward without tears during the most painful moments of 2015, the most terrible year of my life.

About the Author

Maryse Wolinski is a French journalist and writer and widow of the late *Charlie Hebdo* cartoonist Georges Wolinski. She is the author of several stories and novels, including *Georges, If You Knew* and *The Passion of Edith S*. She lives in Paris.